HOBEY BAKER

American Legend

"The Natural" From an early age it was apparent to all who witnessed the graceful athlete that he was something very special. There was no sport that Hobey Baker did not excel at. With his matinee idol looks and his signature blonde hair, the helmet-less Hobey was easily identified by his legions of fans, as he would explode into one of his patented open-field, fearless gridiron runs.

HOBEY BAKER
American Legend

by
Emil R. Salvini

The Hobey Baker Memorial Foundation
Saint Paul, Minnesota

ISBN 0-9763453-0-7

Library of Congress Control Number: 2005921385

FIRST EDITION April 2005

Published by
The Hobey Baker Memorial Foundation
Saint Paul, Minnesota

Attention corporations, schools, and sports organizations: *Hobey Baker: American Legend* is available as a fundraiser, gift, or premium. For additional information contact your local bookstore or the publisher at: info@hobeybaker.net or write, Hobey Baker, Box 4559, Wayne, New Jersey 07470-4559

Printed in the United States of America
Designed by Nancy A. Salvini
All photographs in this publication, unless otherwise credited, are reproduced with permission from the University Archives Department of Rare Books and Special Collections, Princeton University Library.

Dedicated to the memory of my sister

Rosemary "Rosebud" Salvini

1957-2003

Acknowledgements

I would like to thank the following people who have helped make this book possible.

Senator Bill Bradley for his generosity in taking the time out of his busy schedule to write the foreword for the book. Both Charles Scribner III and his son Charles for sharing family memories of St. Paul's, Princeton, and Hobey in the introduction.

Hobey Baker: American Legend would not have gone to press without the Hobey Baker Memorial Foundation. I especially wish to thank Les Larson of the foundation for his time and energy in making the book a reality.

Thanks to Ben Primer of Princeton University for making available the images from the university archives. Thanks to my editor, Sheila Holmes, for sharing her time and expertise.

I would also like to offer a very special thanks to my wife, Nancy, for never failing to inspire and for her steadfast belief in me.

St. Paul's School in Concord, New Hampshire, became a second home for both Hobey and his brother Thornton, when their parents enrolled the boys in the elite school in 1903. Hobey became the living embodiment of the fictional schoolboy, dime-novel hero, Frank Merriwell. Created by George Patten, Merriwell loved country, motherhood, and school, and like Hobey, he placed clean sportsmanship above winning.

Far better it is to dare mighty things, to win glorious triumphs even though checkered by failure, than to rank with those poor spirits who neither enjoy nor suffer much because they live in the gray twilight that knows neither victory nor defeat.

Theodore Roosevelt

FOREWORD

I first learned about Hobey Baker when I was a student athlete at Princeton.

As Princeton's most celebrated athlete of the early twentieth century, he was a genuine superstar on both the ice and gridiron. He is the only individual to be inducted in both the Hockey Hall of Fame and the College Football Hall of Fame. Today the Hobey Baker Memorial Award, awarded to the country's most talented player, is college hockey's equivalent to the Heisman Trophy. Thousands admired the gifted, handsome Princeton athlete including F. Scott Fitzgerald, who patterned several of his memorable characters after Baker.

When the Great War broke out in Europe, Hobey joined the legendary Lafayette Escadrille and took part in deadly air battles alongside Eddie Rickenbacker against the feared Flying Circus of Baron Richthofen, the Red Baron, over the trenches and death fields of France.

Just weeks after the armistice ended the horrific carnage, Baker lost his life in a senseless and mysterious plane crash, his orders to return home discovered tucked in his jacket pocket. He was twenty-six years old. His story is one

of courage, adventure, chivalry and suspense. The Great
War forever shattered America's innocence, and the Hobey
Baker story conveys how fragile life is for all of us.

Senator Bill Bradley
2005

INTRODUCTION

In the pantheon of athletes Hobey Baker deserves a special niche: not only is he the first American elected to the Hockey Hall of Fame, but he is also the only athlete ever enshrined both there and in the College Football Hall of Fame. In the words of his school hockey coach Malcolm Gordon (himself an eventual member of that Hockey Hall of Fame), Baker "set a new standard for amateur sportsmanship and the game is better because of his leadership. No one could play with or against Hobey without being influenced by his spirit of fair play." According to his contemporary Lawrence Perry, he "was qualified to stand alone as the ultimate product of all that is worthy, not only in American college athletics, but in American college life." It is only fitting that the honor bestowed each year on the best American college hockey player is the Hobey Baker Award.

Following my father and grandfather, I had the good fortune of retracing Hobey's footsteps from St. Paul's School in Concord, New Hampshire, southward to Princeton University. Both schools rightly claim him as an alumnus hero, and his spirit still permeates their athletic domains. In the official history of St. Paul's, author August

Heckscher vividly sketches Baker's prodigious talents: "He had extraordinary gifts, backed by a spunky determination that enabled him to do well in studies or in the choir or in whatever sport he tried. In his first-form year, hoisted to the horizontal bar, he promptly executed a giant swing. Putting on roller skates for the first time, he was performing all kinds of spins on one foot after the first few minutes. He played excellent football, won a swimming race, coxed a crew; and in his fourth-form year, at fifteen years of age, he was on the school hockey team. A pleasant recollection finds Hobey Baker as a sixth former getting permission to take 'night flights' with friends. He especially liked to skate at night, racing over the pond's dark surface, carrying a puck on his stick without being able to see it."

By the time Hobey arrived at Princeton as a freshman, the national spotlight had already focused on him. Still he outshone all expectations. Hobey was a friend and contemporary of my grandfather Scribner both at St. Paul's and at Princeton. I have a framed photograph of my family's college eating club, the Ivy Club, where both these blond Adonises may be found posing with their friends outside the front door. In his first novel, *This Side of Paradise*, another contemporary Princetonian and Scribner author, Scott Fitzgerald fictionalized Hobey as seen through the wondering eyes of Amory Blaine: "He sighed eagerly. There at the head of the white platoon marched Allenby, the football captain, slim and defiant, as if aware that this year the hopes of the college rested on him, that his hundred-and-sixty pounds were expected to dodge to victory through the heavy blue and crimson lines."

By the time I arrived at Princeton two generations later, Hobey's portrait, featuring his varsity black sweater with orange P, hung in the entrance hall of Ivy. Across the campus the university's first indoor hockey rink had been built and named in his memory decades earlier. He was such a living legend that when one of my classmates, a varsity hockey player, discovered at dinner one night that his beautiful "blind date" was Hobey's great-niece he decided then and there that he would marry her. And he did. (Their children are indeed fine athletes, confirming his genetic hunch.)

Thanks to Hobey, my Princetonian son Charlie is the youngest published author in our family. Between his freshman and sophomore years he was commissioned to write a biographical essay on Baker for an encyclopedia of sports figures. He did a masterly job of distilling Hobey's achievement—his athletic grace and glamour, his idealism and sportsmanship—into a few pages. But for those who hunger for more, Emil Salvini's magnificent biography—the first in forty years—here provides a literary feast and a full-bodied portrait, placing the legendary star in the context of his age, an era of athletic chivalry we have sadly lost—let us pray not forever. Salvini holds up a mirror to a hero and to an ideal as he reflects revealing light on both.

Charles Scribner III
New York, 2005

Photograph courtesy Charles Scribner III

Charles Scribner, seated bottom row last on right and Hobey Baker top row fifth from left in front of the Ivy Club, circa 1913.

PROLOGUE

On the eleventh hour, of the eleventh day, of the eleventh month of 1918, the signing of the armistice signaled the end of the Great War that had convulsed Europe for over five years and claimed the lives of ten million soldiers. Spontaneous celebrations broke out around the globe as the news spread that the horrific carnage had ended. A Detroit shopkeeper, upon hearing the news, hung a sign in his store window that read, "Closed – Too Happy to Work," and joined the joyous pandemonium taking place in the street.

A little more than a month after the armistice, on a damp, chilly December morning, Captain Hobart A. H. Baker's brief life came to an end, when the fighter plane he was flying solo crashed in the French countryside. Hobey, as he was known to his fans and friends, had been one of America's most famous amateur athletes, a genuine superstar in an era when the eastern establishment Ivy-colleges ruled the national sports scene.

The story of his tragic and pointless death produced worldwide headlines as the press reported, *Hobey Baker Killed in Europe during Last Flight*. It was the type of story the public devoured: *The Prince of Princeton Dead at Age Twenty-six.* Baker's orders to return home were found in his jacket pocket as his broken body was dragged from the crumbled plane. Fighter pilots, especially the ones who had survived the war, learned early on not to tempt fate, and reports indicate that Hobey's men had pleaded with him not to take that unnecessary flight. No one knew for sure why he did, and it remains a mystery today. Opinions differed, but the most popular theory suggested that, before shipping out, the diligent officer felt duty-bound to test a recently repaired airplane and the accident was caused by engine failure. Others suggested a darker motive.

A French newspaper speculated that suicide was a possibility, citing Hobey's recent breakup with his fiancée, a Manhattan debutante, who had broken his heart when she abruptly ended their engagement and accepted another marriage proposal. A close source hinted that with his athletic career behind him and the war over, the dashing athlete and warrior of the sky had nothing else to live for. Naturally, his family, friends and the "old grads" from Princeton felt it was an accident, plain and simple, and that anything else was blasphemy.

Baker was often described by his contemporaries as a blond Adonis. To look at his photograph is to understand these recollections and why F. Scott Fitzgerald, an impressionable Princeton freshman during Hobey's senior year, would later pattern his Allenby character in *This Side of Paradise* after Baker. Describing a parade of "white-shirted, white-trousered" upperclassmen marching up University Place singing Princeton's "Going Back to Nassau Hall," Fitzgerald wrote, "There at the head of the white platoon marched Allenby, the football captain, slim and defiant, as if aware that this year the hopes of the college rested on him, that his hundred-and-sixty pounds were expected to dodge to victory through the heavy blue and crimson lines."

Andrew Turnbull, a Fitzgerald biographer, would later write of Baker's era, "Varsity football players were looked upon as demi-gods, and Hobey Baker, captain of football and star of hockey–someone like Baker loomed so high in the heavens that he was scarcely visible."

Hobey Baker's accomplishments were impressive: he died a decorated World War One hero and is the only athlete enshrined in both the Hockey Hall of Fame and College Football Hall of Fame. He is also the only amateur in both the Canadian and Hockey Halls of Fame and was an All-American twice in football and three times in hockey at Princeton. He was a superb athlete, a "natural" who routinely brought thousands to their feet, as he effortlessly flew down the ice or football field. A classmate who watched Hobey play hockey in 1914 recalled almost fifty years later that he had never seen a human being move so fast under his own power. Hobey Baker was one of those rarities who played for the pure love of the game.

In an era when the gentleman athlete defined sports and collegiate athletics was viewed as modern chivalry, Baker was the ideal of his age, an Ivy-League prince. He played by "the code" of fairness and would have abhorred today's win-at-all-cost philosophy in sports. Hobey shunned publicity and was universally respected for his sportsmanship, modesty, and civility on and off the playing field. It is said that winners like Hobey Baker never knew they were in a race; they just loved to run.

The inscription on his tombstone reads:

You seemed winged, even as a lad,
With that swift look of those who know the sky,
It was no blundering fate that stooped and bade
You break your wings, and fall to earth and die,
I think some day you may have flown too high,
So the immortals saw you and were glad,
Watching the beauty of your spirits flame,
Until they loved and called you, and you came.

Had Hobey Baker not existed, some clever word-smith would have been compelled to create him. Baker was the stuff of legends. There were his brilliant feats of athleticism on the ice and gridiron, his daring deeds flying with the celebrated Lafayette Flying Corps during World War One, and his mysterious, tragic death at such a young age. It was evident early in his life that the gods so loved Hobey that they endowed him with abilities that could thrill and astonish his fellow mortals, and in the end, like the mythical Icarus, he flew too close to the sun and fell from the sky, giving birth to his legend.

Schoolmates of Hobey recalled how on early autumn evenings at St. Paul's, he was always the first to seek out the black ice on Turkey Pond where, at lightning speed, he fled the few friends who could keep up with him on his night flights.

"they are different from you and me..."

F. Scott Fitzgerald, *The Rich Boy*

Chapter One

What is undeniable is that Hobey Baker deeply touched all those who crossed his path. Dr. Lay Martin, a 1914 Princeton classmate of Baker, poignantly wrote in 1963, "It is strange that after all these years his memory still haunts me." Another contemporary attended prep school with Hobey and as a Yale undergraduate played ice hockey against Baker and the Princeton team. He remembered years later, "...after nearly a half century Hobey's personality is as clear as if we had known him yesterday." He boasted that while he had the good fortune during a long career to meet and interact with cabinet-level statesmen and many of the industrial giants of his era, he never forgot Baker, adding, "Here was a boy who died nearly a half century ago and everyone who knew him has a vivid recollection of what he said and did."

Hobart Amory Hare Baker was born during America's Gilded Age to an affluent family in Bala-Cynwyd, Pennsylvania on January 15, 1892. Popular nineteenth century author and social activist, Edward Bellamy wrote of that period, "We breed two great classes – paupers and millionaires," and the Bakers were prosperous, prominent members of upper class Philadelphia society. Bala-Cynwyd, located on the prestigious Philadelphia Main Line, enabled middle- and upper-class families like the Bakers to move from the once desirable and now congested commercial Philadelphia city center to the suburbs. The picturesque towns that comprised the Main Line, towns with equally picturesque Welsh names like Bryn Mawr, Bala-Cynwyd, Merion and Berwyn, developed between the mid-nineteenth and early twentieth century as the Pennsylvania Railroad pushed its "main line" westward from Philadelphia. Prosperous families were lured from the city to the lush, green "street car suburbs," and for the first time in history a person could easily commute between a job in the city and a country home. Each new Main Line station created another town, and prominent Philadelphians employed stylish architects such as Frank Furness and Addison Hutton to create their suburban country estates.

Hobey's father, A. Thornton Baker or "Bobby" as he was known to his friends, had played football for Princeton, his father's and uncle's alma mater, and after graduation was successful enough in the plush upholstery business to settle into a comfortable country club lifestyle. Bobby was prominent in Philadelphia's Main Line society and an active member of numerous clubs including the ultra-exclusive Fish House Club, the oldest sporting organization in North America. His wife, mother to Hobey and older brother Thornton, was May Augusta Pemberton, an elegant Philadelphia society belle with the appropriate pedigree. Hobey's maternal uncle and namesake, Dr. Hobart Amory Hare, was the president of the respected Jefferson Medical Hospital and the presiding physician at Hobey's birth.

Hobey and Thornton Baker enjoyed the insulated, privileged childhood that only wealth and breeding could provide, barely noticing that the world around them was rapidly changing. While they spent summers in Europe or Newport, Rhode Island, half of Philadelphia's students routinely abandoned school by age 14, and one-fifth of children between the ages of 10 and 14 held jobs.

This was a time of class division and labor unrest. Both deepened as a worldwide financial panic and depression began in 1893 and lasted until 1897. Businesses began to fail, and by the winter of 1893-1894 over 2,500,000 American workers were unemployed. In stark contrast to the misery of the under class, social arbiter Ward McAllister amused the country when he coined the phrase *the 400*, declaring that there were "only 400 people in fashionable New York Society" important enough to be invited to an Astor affair. In truth, the Astor ballroom could only accommodate four hundred people; but no matter, the phrase stuck. McAllister had earlier declared that being a millionaire was a distinct profession.

Embarrassed by the widening class division, apologists for the monied set took Charles Darwin's theories of the survival of the fittest in nature and applied them to human society. Social Darwinists, as they became known, believed that the weak would fail while the robust Anglo-Saxon aristocracy would always rise to the top. Faculty members at Harvard and Yale routinely lectured that although social evolution might seem cruel, it was a necessary and inevitable process and to meddle with it would prove fruitless. The *Gospel of Wealth,* authored by industrialist Andrew Carnegie in 1889, conveniently preached that the concentration of wealth in the hands of a few industrialists was "essential to the future of the race."

On January 1, 1892, fourteen days before Hobey's birth, a seemingly insignificant event took place that would soon deepen the division between classes and threaten the ruling aristocracy. The New York Bay receiving station, Ellis Island, opened for business, and before closing in 1954 it would eventually process twenty million immigrants, all searching for the Baker dream. These were not the "old immigrants" from Germany, Scandinavia and the British Isles whom Americans had grown comfortable with and who comprised three quarters of the immigrants before 1880.

These were the "new immigrants" from Italy, Russia, Austria-Hungary, Turkey, Greece, and Poland.

The rapid industrialization that took place in the late
nineteenth century cried out for inexpensive, unskilled im-
migrant labor, yet the social Darwinists felt threatened and
feared that the steady stream of foreigners rapidly filling
the East coast cities might somehow "pollute" the Anglo-
Saxon race and weaken its physical status.

This fear was intensified by a feeling that "the man
of action," who came into being during the Civil War, was
being transformed into a "man of business," trapped in his
cramped office, growing more effeminate each day. The
popular fiction of the day filled the heads of desk-bound
warriors with a desire to demonstrate their imagined Saxon
chivalry. Robust men would be required to stand up to the
immigrants, union organizers, anarchists, and the hoards
of "undesirables" who disembarked daily on places like Ellis Island. The peculiar concept of the muscular Christian
was born out of this concern: a new man of action who not
only excelled in academics, but could prove superior in the
athletic arena and stand up to this feared infusion of foreign blood.

Dudley A. Sargent, who joined Harvard University in
1879 as director of the Hemenway Gymnasium, addressed
this threat of immigration by promoting the "gentleman
athlete" at Harvard and the other eastern establishment
universities. He believed physical development was closely
tied to moral improvement and that the gentleman athlete
would "bear his burdens in the world, and help to advance
the condition of the rest of mankind by improving the stock
and raising the average." Sargent's lessons were not lost on
Theodore Roosevelt, a Harvard undergraduate at the time,
who would later ascend to the presidency of the United
States. Roosevelt was the embodiment of the "man of action" and a proponent of athletics as a way to prepare students for the strenuous competition of the world. As president, he would later come to the defense of college football

on numerous occasions when movements to ban the brutal sport gained momentum. He once said in a speech at Harvard that he did not object to a sport because it was rough and did not believe in seeing Harvard, "turn out molly-coddles instead of vigorous men." Others, like the Boston patrician and Harvard alumnus Henry Cabot Lodge, took sports a step further and spoke of gentlemanly athletics as a substitute and a preparation for war. Concerning the brutality of the sport – thirty players nationwide lost their lives in one year alone – Lodge reminded his aristocratic friends that the injuries incurred on the playing field were, after all, "part of the price which the English speaking race had paid for being world-conquerors."

Up to this time, spectator sports in America had been limited to the fledgling baseball league and pastimes inherited from the English such as horse racing, cockfighting, prize fighting, and rugby style football games. While America's golden age of sports would not occur until the 1920s, intercollegiate football took center stage during the last twenty years of the nineteenth century and provided an entertainment-starved public and a hungry press with events like the annual Yale-Harvard game, held on Thanksgiving Day and frequently attended by over 70,000 fans. The Harvard-Yale contest became known as "The Game," and in 1900 it generated revenues of over $40,000. Here was an opportunity to see the cream of the eastern colleges prove their manhood in bloody battles akin to miniature war games.

The physical appearance of the gentleman athlete and a new definition of the ideal American were fleshed out in 1895 by illustrator Charles Dana Gibson. His depiction of the perfect woman, the Gibson Girl, was a slim, cool, aloof beauty with a pompadour hairstyle. Her male escort, fashioned after Gibson himself, was a clean-shaven, square-jawed specimen with broad shoulders who required no padding in his jacket.

The concepts of muscular Christianity and social

Darwinism were further advanced in 1898 when the United States flexed its muscles and struck a blow for "Manifest Destiny" and national glory, defeating the Spanish in Cuba while acquiring Guam, Puerto Rico and the Philippine Islands in the bargain. While sports provided a remedy for the soft, indoor Gilded Age American, the ultimate antidote was war. Theodore Roosevelt took a step closer to the New York governor's mansion and eventually the presidency when he and his Rough Riders gained fame during the war in their celebrated charge up Kettle Hill near Santiago, Cuba. As Harvard's Sargent had accurately predicted, the amateur athlete was bearing his burdens in the world. Ten of Roosevelt's Rough Riders listed their occupation as amateur "football player."

With Gibson's illustrations adorning the popular press and inter-collegiate athletics gaining nationwide popularity, the stage was set for the quintessential gentleman athlete, one who would someday captivate the country's imagination.

St. Paul's

The marriage of Bobby and May Baker was rapidly unraveling when they decided in 1903 to enroll Hobey and Thornton in the exclusive St. Paul's School in Concord, New Hampshire. The couple stayed together for several more years but eventually divorced in 1907. Years later, a New York newspaper callously noted in Hobey's engagement announcement, "The present Mrs. Alfred Baker is not the mother of Hobart, his mother having been the beautiful but frivolous former May Pemberton, who managed to keep the Quaker City gossips in a turmoil for many years before she and Alfred were finally separated for all times by the divorce courts." Considering the era and the conservative Episcopalian Main Line culture, the scandal must have been substantial and the effect on the two young boys immeasurable. Reports indicate that the Baker brothers were all but abandoned by their preoccupied, feuding parents and forced to rely on the kindness of relatives and the staff of St. Paul's, their extended family for the next seven years.

The decision to send the boys to St. Paul's was probably two-fold. It was the prep school of choice for many Philadelphia Main Line families and the growing ruling social elite. The first of the American church schools, established in 1855 as one of the "feeder" schools for the big three eastern colleges, St. Paul's was the model for other prep schools such as St. Mark's, Middlesex, St. George's and Groton, all patterned after Britain's legendary public schools, Eton, Harrow, and Rugby.

The second reason was of a more personal nature. Several of Bobby Baker's cousins had attended St. Paul's, and one of his cousins, James Conover, was a master at the school. Conover's wife, Mary, was the daughter of the first rector of the school and was to become a surrogate mother to Hobey and Thornton. Their second cousin, J. P. Conover, Jr., remembered Hobey and Thornton arriving at St. Paul's as, "….two sturdy little boys in short trousers and Eton collars, Hobart with very light hair, almost towheaded." Their cousin recalled that although the boys were neglected by their natural mother and uprooted from their childhood home, they "were treated always as members of the family and Mother had to look after them as such, their clothes, manners, etc." Mary Conover was a beautiful, good-natured woman and excelled at comforting her homesick charges. In the time they spent at the school, in Hobey's case from age eleven to eighteen, the Conovers and the St. Paul's staff were the Baker boys' family, and after graduation Hobey's closest friendships would be the ones forged at St. Paul's. Hobey's personality took shape at the school, and both he and his brother must have been deeply affected by their parents' breakup and more importantly, by their mother's abandonment of them. While comprehensive studies of the impact of divorce on children were decades away, the facts then were the same as now. When asked to rate a number of life events in terms of stressfulness, the only thing children rank as more stressful than parental divorce is the death of a parent or close family member. Another study found that children who are allied with their same-sex parent, as was Hobey with his father and on a larger scale the masculine culture of St. Paul's, tend to develop chauvinistic tendencies and are often alienated from the opposite sex. A fellow student at the school remembered him as being somewhat introverted. More significantly, the friend wrote of Hobey, "While he was admired and respected I think, as I look back, the thing he really wanted more than anything else was to love (but I am not sure he knew exactly how to express it) and in turn to be loved." This schoolboy's observation seems prophetic as Hobey searched for but never found a woman's love during his short life.

St. Paul's was the training ground at that time for the boys of the American aristocracy. In 1893 a local New Hampshire newspaper noted that Cornelius Vanderbilt and his entourage had arrived in their city by private railroad car to visit his grandson, a St. Paul's student and one of several Vanderbilts who attended the school during the late nineteenth and early twentieth century. St. Paul's application list included the likes of the Morgans and Mellons, all interested in enrolling their sons in the exclusive school. Their lives followed similar paths: young boy at prep school, followed by university student at Harvard, Princeton, or Yale and finally on to the life of an upper-class, well-connected "old-boy" of business, government or the law. The prep school was not designed to foster creative thinking in students but instead sought to produce conformity. Author Arthur Stanwood Pier noted in his book, *St. Paul's School 1855-1934*, that St.Paul's preferred boys with the right attitude and school spirit and that cheerful conformity to regulations was expected of them. He later observed that if parents desired a school to teach their sons to think like other people, St. Paul's provided the perfect answer.

A natural outlet for the students at St. Paul's was sports including cricket, football, crew, baseball and hockey. It was believed that athletics would instill in the young boys a sense of the true gentleman and sportsman, and these activities became an integral part of the educational experience. In *St. Paul's School in the Great War,* published by the school's alumni association in 1918, the authors tell the story of a young World War One soldier, a St. Paul's alumnus, who lay dying of combat wounds in a hospital in Europe. When asked by the nurse why he, an American, had entered the war before his country had, he whispered to her, "Our fight, too." The authors went on to speak of the curriculum at the school and to note that while football and Latin may seem unrelated, ".....the end and purpose of them is the same; they merge and send out into life just such another boy....he who dying said so briefly and quietly, "Our fight too." The lessons were well taught. Inspired by their *noblesse oblige,* their noble obligation, forty- eight of St. Paul's "old boys" lost their lives in the Great War, a dramatically high number for a small prep school.

Hobey proved to be a more than adequate student at St. Paul's, but it was sports that presented the opportunity for the young boy to gain self-esteem and attention, both sorely lacking in children of divorce. His masters and fellow students quickly observed that Hobey had been blessed with extraordinary athletic ability. His cousin recalled Hobey's powerful swimming ability and how he would move through the water, "like some sort of engine." He seemed to effortlessly excel at anything he attempted. Like John Knowles's bigger than life character Phineas in his novel *A Separate Peace,* Hobey played sports with such ease and inborn skill that a casual observer might mistakenly believe that he too could master the game in a weekend. With only a friend present, Phineas nonchalantly broke the school swimming record and then forced the awestruck friend to keep his accomplishment a secret.

Another student remembered how he introduced

Hobey to golf while at St. Paul's. "I had played, not well, for years, yet Hobey beat me the first time we played, getting in the forties on the short nine-hole course they had at the school." Stories abound of how he executed a flawless 360-degree turn the first time he tried the school's horizontal bar or how after strapping on a pair of roller skates for the first time, he performed stunts on just one leg in a matter of minutes. His legend at the school grew.

St. Paul's had a gifted cross-country runner who eventually went on to some fame at Yale. A student remembered that Hobey entered the school's annual race, "just for the fun of it," and won easily. He was powerfully built, of medium height with broad shoulders, narrow hips and a level of coordination that few possessed. Most of his schoolmates' memories consist primarily of his athletic achievements and the modesty that accompanied them. "To me he was someone greatly admired and to be copied whenever possible – a very boy among boys," remembered one classmate. Another friend recalled that Hobey either said something kind about another student or said nothing, and while he quickly developed into a school hero, he "never strutted nor was he a snob." Hobey seemed to be the living embodiment of author George Patten's popular dime-novel figure, Frank Merriwell. Patten wrote 20,000 words a week for the *Tip Top Weekly* and created Merriwell as the personification of the clean-cut, ideal, turn-of-the-century American boy. Merriwell loved his country, motherhood, and school and like Hobey, placed clean sportsmanship above winning.

As St. Paul's number one athlete, Hobey was recruited by Bogi, one of the school's two secret societies, both patterned after Yale's furtive college societies. The second group, Hoi, derived its name from *hoi aretoi,* meaning "the best," and both societies were reserved for St. Paul's connected elite. The masters, after attempting for years to force them to disband, eventually turned a blind eye to these groups. They could not expel a boy discovered to be a member because as school historian Arthur Stanwood

Pier later wrote, "Some of the best and most influential boys were members...."

Their activities consisted primarily of political shenanigans such as stuffing the ballot boxes during school elections to gain an advantage over one another, and more ominously in the Hoi's case, marking a new member by pressing a hot penny to his stomach. Members were assessed twenty-five cents a week to keep the group well stocked with the popular magazines of the day and contraband items such as alcohol and cigarettes. Hobey discovered early on that his athletic prowess gained him entry into a world traditionally reserved for the Vanderbilts and the Morgans.

Football, baseball, and crew all paled at St. Paul's in comparison to ice hockey, a sport that had achieved secular religious status at the small New Hampshire prep school and for good reason. Historians of the popular sport believe that hockey was first introduced in the United States by St. Paul's in the last decades of the nineteenth-century, eventually spreading via alumni to the eastern colleges then to club teams across America.

As far back as the 1860's, a primitive form of the game, a sort of ice shinny, was played on the school's Turkey Pond, when on still New England nights, the pond would freeze as smooth as glass and create what the students fondly referred to as "black ice." Shinny was an informal affair; the school would divide into two halves and skate a wooden block across the frozen pond with primitive wooden sticks. The first snows of December would cover the ponds and bring the activities to an abrupt conclusion until the school solved the problem by constructing its first of nine artificial rinks in 1885.

The true beginning of the modern game took place in 1880 when St. Paul's schoolmaster, J. P. Conover, traveled to Montreal on a business trip and returned to the school with several field hockey-type sticks and an octagonal block covered with leather. Malcolm K. Gordon, later known as the "father of American hockey," joined the school as coach, and by 1885, hockey had become a recognized sport at St. Paul's. Gordon is credited with establishing many of the rules that would evolve into modern hockey. The school took hockey seriously, and since St. Paul's had no traditional hockey rival at the time, students based much of their athletic activity on club and intramural competition. Clubs named Delphian, Old Hundreds and Isthmian battled each other for bragging rights, and today represent some of the oldest athletic clubs in America.

As fate would have it, Hobey's hockey career at St. Paul's began the same time the modern sport was taking shape. Improvements in equipment and new rules had produced a much faster, more exciting game. His natural ability lent itself to the new sport, and as with anything athletic, Hobey excelled. A fellow student vividly recalled more than fifty years later, "It was always Hobey who first in the autumn scented black ice on the Turkey ponds where, at lightning speed, he led the few friends who could keep up with him on night flights." It was during these late night skating sessions that Hobey developed the magical ability to carry the puck along the ice while never looking down at his stick.

Another friend remembered bone-chilling nights on the moonlit pond when the students practiced puck handling and someone would suddenly notice Hobey effortlessly skating the puck at breakneck speed from one end of the ice to the other, never looking down. "I believe he could just naturally feel it and imagine where it was ahead of him," the friend recalled. It became apparent to the students and masters that the little, blond-haired boy from the broken Main Line family was something special.

In the early 1890s, several wealthy St. Paul's alumni, eager to continue playing the game after college but faced with limited opportunities, purchased the old St. Nicholas Ice Company on 66th Street in Manhattan and built the St. Nicholas Rink. The home team, the St. Nick's, consisted primarily of former Ivy League hockey players, and in addition to playing competing clubs like the Irish-American

Athletic Club or the Wanderers, would each year challenge their old college teams.

St. Paul's School later began the practice of renting the St. Nicholas arena for an annual Christmas holiday hockey game against prep school rivals. In 1908, the St. Paul's boys were scheduled to skate against the Lawrenceville, New Jersey team. The game was always a festive event and an opportunity for the alumni of the schools, most of them either Ivy League students or grads, to get together, renew friendships, and cheer their old prep school team to victory.

That particular year had been a tough one for New York sports fans. Many were still in shock after their beloved Giants baseball team barely missed playing in the 1908 World Series because of one of the most disputed incidents in baseball. The deciding game of the National League pennant race, played at the Polo Grounds against the Chicago Cubs, was tied 1-1 in the bottom of the ninth inning. It appeared that the Giants had scored the winning run and were going to the World Series when their player hit safely to center field. Unfortunately, Fred Merkle, the Giants' runner on first base, failed to advance to second base when he saw the winning run score. Believing the game was over, he walked toward the clubhouse, essentially invalidating the run. As the Cubs' second baseman tried to retrieve the ball and tag Merkle out, the crazed fans mobbed the field and a near riot broke out. It was later ruled that the game was a tie. The Cubs eventually captured the pennant and advanced to the World Series after winning a special post-season playoff game against the Giants. The irate New York fans invented the terms "bonehead" and "boner" when referring to Merkle's mistake, and these terms are now part of American slang lexicon.

The city's sportswriters were searching for a new story that would electrify the big town and, if only for a few days, help the fans forget the Giants' fiasco and Merkle's bonehead error. An epidemic and a golden-haired prep school boy were about to oblige them. It appeared that St. Paul's would have to cancel the annual holiday game and absorb a substantial financial loss when the Lawrenceville team was forced to drop out of the game because of a scarlet fever epidemic. The "old boys" came to the rescue when the St. Nick's team agreed to play the schoolboys. The story quickly captivated the city. A schoolboy team was about to take on New York's champion St. Nick's, a powerful hockey team composed of ex-Ivy League stars and several Canadian semi-pros.

The fans, the old grads, and the New York press were treated to a game few would forget as Hobey Baker and the St. Paul's team took to the ice against the older, rugged men. The crowd roared as the young boys carried the play to the St. Nick's over and over again, and though in the end a victory was not to be, the press reported that the youngsters outplayed the veterans through most of the tilt. Hobey realized that he was a long way from Turkey Pond as his lightning speed, gifted skating and hockey wizardry would time after time bring the jaded New York crowd to its feet. The New York press had found its story, and at age sixteen, Hobey Baker had his first taste of fame.

The St. Paul's team would regularly play the Ivy universities in friendly matches, to hone their skills, test their plays and give the colleges a chance to catch a glimpse of next year's crop of hockey talent. In one year alone, the captains of the Harvard, Yale and Princeton teams were all St. Paul's grads, and the Yale champion freshman team consisted entirely of St. Paul's boys. The tiny New Hampshire prep school had become an incubator for future collegiate hockey stars.

In 1907 the Princeton varsity team captured the intercollegiate title, but the celebration was muted by the fact that Hobey Baker and his schoolboy chums had defeated the Tigers, 4-0, earlier in the season. A year earlier Baker had dealt the same hand to Harvard, when he effortlessly overtook their speedy captain, stripped him of the puck time after time, and sent the dejected Crimson squad back to the locker room with a 7-5 loss.

Back at St. Paul's, Thornton and Hobey flourished, and both hoped to uphold the Baker family tradition and attend Princeton University when their time came. Thornton, who had spent his childhood and St. Paul's years in his younger brother's shadow, eagerly anticipated beginning college in 1908. Sadly, it was not meant to be, and Thornton's time in the sun never came. In 1907, America entered its twentieth depression since 1790, and Hobey and Thornton's recently remarried father was forced to deliver some sobering news to his sons. There was not enough money to send both boys to college and a choice had to be made. In Thornton's mind, the choice was simple. He gallantly and unselfishly deferred to Hobey, skipping college to go to work to help put his gifted brother through school. While the elite eastern universities sent delegations to St. Paul's to lure Hobey to attend their schools, Thornton left the Ivy world and all that it promised for a world of time clocks and assembly lines. The brothers had depended on each other since the day their troubled parents sent the two little boys away to school, and Hobey once again had to depend on his older brother. He would remember his brother's sacrifice for the remainder of his life. Some sixty years after the incident, a fellow St. Paul's student recalled Thornton's generosity and feared that too little had been said of it. He believed that Thornton had "the finest boy's voice in the school choir" and could still envision him as a young boy, "singing appropriately, 'O for the Wings, for the Wings of a Dove'."

Hobey's family decided to have him stay on for an extra year at St. Paul's. Boys in those days often "prepped" for an additional year before entering college. In Hobey's case, grades were not the issue; he was an above average student. What was more likely, considering his father's financial condition, was that another year would mean more money for college. In addition to the financial concerns, his school masters anticipated that he would quickly become involved in college hockey and football, sports that were particularly brutal and dangerous in those days. In 1909, Hobey's final year at St. Paul's and the year that he should have begun college, twenty-six deaths occurred on football fields nationwide, an astonishingly high number considering that the sport was in its infancy and had not approached the popularity it enjoys today. Another year would afford the seventeen-year-old the opportunity to mature physically and possibly prevent a serious injury down the line.

In the meantime, stories were spreading throughout the college world of the talented young man who at fifteen had received the St. Paul's award for best athlete, excelling at hockey, football, baseball, tennis, swimming and track.

The 1908-1909 St. Paul's team that played against the mighty St. Nick's in Manhattan in the winter of 1908. Hobey, captain of the schoolboy team, is fourth from the left, and his brother, Thornton, is on his right. The game pitted boys against men and was the first glimpse the public got of the gifted athlete. It was love at first sight.

Tiger, Tiger, Burning Bright…

William Blake, *The Tiger*

Chapter Two

Hobey Baker began his meteoric rise to stardom in 1910, the same year Halley's Comet passed so close to the earth that its dazzling, fiery tail could be seen across much of the North American night sky. While thousands of men and women across the country purchased bogus "comet pills" to protect them from the mysterious, unearthly traveler, and others hid in cyclone cellars and caves fearing that the world was going to end, a bright new world was about to present itself to young Hobey. He was one of the fortunate four percent of the population who had the opportunity to attend college, and as a gifted athlete, Baker had his choice of schools. By the time Hobey was beginning college, the big three – Harvard, Yale and Princeton – and their fledgling rivals had discovered that there was money to be made in athletics. In addition, university reputations were on the line and administrators began to realize to their dismay that the wealthiest, brightest and most influential students wanted to attend colleges with winning teams. After attending a Princeton-Harvard game where the Princeton end, Sam White, blocked a field goal and ran ninety-five yards for the winning touchdown, an impressionable F. Scott Fitzgerald wrote in his scrapbook next to the prized ticket stub, "Sam White decides me for Princeton." This was also the first game in which Hobey played for Princeton as a sophomore, and it was the beginning of Fitzgerald's lifetime admiration of the heroic athlete. As he began his freshman year at Old Nassau, Fitzgerald wired his mother to send his football pads and shoes immediately. Unfortunately, football was not to be for the slightly built Fitzgerald, and he would spend his entire life regretting his lack of athletic prowess.

Although the presidents and faculty of the elite eastern universities vehemently opposed recruiting students based on their athletic ability, at least publicly, boosters and alumni were not beyond some gentle and often, not so gentle, persuasion. Many a boy who demonstrated gridiron ability was provided with tuition or some form of financial assistance by alumni organizations to attend St. Paul's, Exeter or Andover, the "feeder" prep schools for the big three. Stories abound about several rather large boys who prepped at some of the better schools, like a future Yale football captain who entered Exeter at twenty-three years of age or another pigskin prodigy who entered at twenty-one. Most of these young men were from working class families and had been lured to these elite schools by alumni and athletic booster clubs and by promises of jobs to earn money for tuition.

Princeton academics were embarrassed by the likes of Charles Patterson, an on-again, off-again student who was known for his aggressive recruiting tactics. Patterson had dropped out of his beloved Princeton toward the end of the nineteenth century to devote all of his time to attracting the best athletes to Old Nassau. He was jokingly referred to as Princeton's oldest living undergraduate when he eventually re-enrolled in the university and somehow managed to obtain a master's degree in 1901. Patterson knew or invented many of the dirty tricks used to recruit ineligible students. Author John Sayle Watterson noted in his book, *College Football – history – spectacle – controversy*, that Patterson had once arranged for over thirty Andover students, most too young to even attend college, to take the Princeton entrance exam. When one of the larger boys was asked by the Princeton monitor why he had taken the exam at his young age, he replied, "Well, Professor, at the top of my paper I wrote my weight – 205 pounds. I guess I'll pass all right. Patterson said I would."

Princeton was trendy among the wealthiest families of Pennsylvania, and the state ranked second in alumni only to New York during Baker's era. In Hobey Baker's case he was academically and financially qualified to attend Princeton or the other eastern establishment schools, and his choice to attend Old Nassau was based on his family's connection to the university. This is not to say that the Princeton boosters did not keep a watchful eye on him during his St. Paul's years. They sent envoys to New Hampshire to protect their interests whenever another school paid Hobey a visit, but their vigilance proved unnecessary; there was never a doubt that he would attend Old Nassau. Baker was the quintessential "legacy;" his father, uncle, grandfather and great-uncle, – a minister of Princeton's Trinity Church in 1909 – had all graduated from Princeton and Hobey had spent many happy days visiting family in the sleepy college hamlet. In addition, his father and uncle had played football for the Tigers, and as one of Hobey's contemporaries observed in 1916, "For a son of a great player to go anywhere else than his father's college would be rank heresy." It was quite common for groups of boys from one prep school to enroll en-masse at the same university and continue their old school ties throughout college and after graduation. Princeton's reputation in the early twentieth century was that of a pleasant country club where the gentleman's *C* was still a respectable grade. Amory Blaine, Fitzgerald's thinly disguised autobiographical character, describes his love of Princeton in *This Side of Paradise*, "...I think of Princeton as being lazy and good-looking and aristocratic - you know, like a spring day." The image of Hobey Baker appears in one form or another in Fitzgerald's imagination and writings. In *This Side of Para-*

dise he borrows Hobey's middle name, Amory, for Amory Blaine. Fitzgerald's deep admiration for his fellow Princetonian is understandable when you consider that towards the end of his life he wrote that his two deepest regrets were that he had never fought overseas in World War One and that he had never become a football hero. He sadly noted that he would often awake from the same dream in which he had achieved these goals. While his football regrets may sound trivial by today's standards, the Ivy League gridiron stars of Baker's and Fitzgerald's era had been elevated to mythical heights by the popular press of the day. The success of the university year was based on the outcome of the Princeton-Yale or Princeton-Harvard game.

The story of John Prentiss Poe, Jr. demonstrates the significance of football in the collegiate culture of the day. A relation of Edgar Allan Poe, John had been one of six brothers to play football for Princeton at the turn of the century. He once said that he believed that war was the greatest game on earth and in 1914 joined the Black Watch, the famed Scotch Regiment, to fight in the Great War while his country waited on the sidelines. He lost the game of his life in France in 1915 during the bloody Battle of Loos. In a ceremony at Princeton honoring his bravery, the teary-eyed speaker told the mourners that Poe "represented the *highest ideals of American football,* not only in life, but in his death upon the battlefields of France." The speaker and audience believed that football was a miniature war game and that Poe's bravery on the battlefield had only been fully developed on the gridiron. Fitzgerald would write of Poe's death, "The death of Johnny Poe with the Black Watch in Flanders starts the cymbals crashing for me, plucks the strings of nervous violins as no adventure of the mind that Princeton ever offered."

Hobey's freshman class entered Princeton in 1910, the same year that its scholarly president, Woodrow Wilson, resigned to try his hand at politics. Wilson had a love affair with Princeton that began in his days as a student. He was a member of the Class of 1879, a distinguished group that contained a future president of the United States, an associate justice of the United States Supreme Court, a governor of Puerto Rico and a director of the New York Life Insurance Company. This closely knit class remained connected throughout their lives and took a strong interest in each other's well being. *The New York Times* in a 1914 story about Wilson attending his class reunion reported that "...if any member gets into trouble a series of telegrams brings hasty response. If anything were to happen to any one and his sons were left un-provided for, the rest of the class would see that his sons went through Princeton." Such was their commitment to Old Nassau.

In spite of this old boy comradeship, it was a public battle over one of Princeton's elite institutions that disillusioned Wilson and eventually contributed to his leaving in 1910 to run for governor of New Jersey. Woodrow Wilson had begun his tenure as president of Princeton in 1902 and to his credit was never afraid to take on the monied class when he deemed it necessary. His reputation as university president had grown in stature. In 1905 he introduced Princeton to the preceptorial method of teaching, an adaptation of Oxford's tutorial system. Always a believer in independent reading rather than course texts and lectures, Wilson introduced a Socratic system consisting of a preceptor leading a small group of students in stimulating discussions based on their independent reading. He boldly hired forty-seven men with the rank of special professor and the special function of preceptor. The plan proved to be more successful than even Wilson had imagined, and the method is still in use at Princeton today. Historians regard the preceptorial system as Wilson's greatest gift to the university. Unfortunately, another of Wilson's plans would not be received with as much enthusiasm.

Social Darwinism had reached its peak at Princeton in the early twentieth century systems with the proliferation of the university's unique eating club tradition.

Although fraternities had been banned at Princeton since 1855, a system of social selection manifested itself toward the end of the nineteenth century in the form of elite eating clubs. These clubs evolved because in the late eighteenth and early nineteenth centuries, Princeton had no system in place to feed its residential students. University officials encouraged and later insisted that their students fend for themselves, and most began taking their meals in the modest boarding houses spread throughout the small town. As time passed, casual eating clubs were formed, and several of these later developed into exclusive clubs. The first, Ivy Club, was formed in 1878, and its members built a grand Queen Anne style house on Prospect Street. Others followed with names like Cottage, Tiger Inn, and Cap and Gown. The clubs built handsome homes on Prospect Street in varying architectural styles, and soon sixteen beautiful structures lined the street.

When university officials finally got around to feeding their students, they limited the service for economic reasons to freshmen and sophomores; the upperclassmen would have to continue fending for themselves. The clubs quickly developed into a system of social selection that rivaled any of the fraternal organizations in other universities. Princeton's reputation as a country club university grew from outsiders' perceptions of these eating clubs. Fitzgerald wrote of the clubs in *This Side of Paradise*, "Ivy, detached and breathlessly aristocratic; Cottage, an impressive melange of brilliant adventurers and well-dressed philanderers; Tiger Inn, broad-shouldered and athletic, vitalized by an honest elaboration of prep-school standards; Cap and Gown, anti-alcoholic, faintly religious and politically powerful..."

The elite, older established "big clubs" like Ivy and Cottage chose the cream of the student body such as the winning athletes and socially prominent, while the other clubs settled for those who did not make that year's social register. Hobey would effortlessly glide into Ivy when his time came to join a club. In a letter written in 1939 to a family friend regarding her son's choice of clubs, F. Scott Fitzgerald advised, "...it would be better for Andrew's future if he joined one of the so-called 'big clubs' at Princeton than one of the others. They are called big not because they necessarily have more members, but because they divide among themselves the leadership in most undergraduate policy." Unfortunately, about one quarter of the sophomore class each year was not considered "clubbable," and these students were left to fend for themselves as they entered their junior year. The clubs had an interesting manner of recruiting members. The selection process, "bickering," defined as "any talk, argument, or discussion designed to induce any man to join any club" took place in late February in what became known as bicker week. During this period, second term sophomores wishing to join a club would anxiously wait in their rooms hoping that the desired club representatives would pay them a bicker call. Fitzgerald counseled his friend regarding her son, "If a delegation of Cottage boys calls on him, he might at least exchange appraising glances with them." It was considered bad form for sophomores to campaign or even bring up the subject of membership to club members during their underclassmen years. Unfortunately, many a distraught student sat alone waiting for a visit that never came. Some lamented that they were forced to settle for a second or third choice; others, sadly, were rejected by all of the clubs. Why a student was excluded was often a mystery. Fitzgerald accurately described the quirky process in *This Side of Paradise,* "...unknown men were elevated into importance when they received certain coveted bids; others who were considered 'all set' found that they had made unexpected enemies, felt themselves stranded and deserted, talked wildly of leaving college." The power of the blackball could doom a man to spending his last two years of college in social obscurity.

Woodrow Wilson fought one of his most memorable battles against the students and alumni of the university over the Prospect Street clubs. Early on in his term as president, he realized the inequity of the eating club system. Not only did it cause division among the students, it was obvious that the rules concerning bicker week were not being adhered to, and since many connected students were chosen for an elite club as early as prep school, it was not unusual for a contingent of Andover or St. Paul's boys to join a select club en masse.

Wilson's answer to the club dilemma was the Quad Plan that he proposed in 1907. In this system, students would be divided into quadrangles where he envisioned they would interact with resident faculty members while having a place to take their meals. He further angered the members of Ivy and the rest of the clubs by suggesting that the existing clubs be incorporated into the Quad system.

His proposal caused a tumult with the elite club members and more importantly with the wealthy alumni who held their clubs sacred. Students were not permitted to stay overnight in their clubs, but alumni members could use the house as a home away from home whenever they visited Old Nassau. Wilson accused the alumni of making snobs of their sons, and they retaliated by closing their checkbooks. Contributions to the university came to a halt, and the ambitious plan died a quick death. This loss, along with a battle over the location of a new graduate school facility, convinced Wilson that it was time to move on. The acrimony was such that during the 1912 presidential election, *The New York Times* ran a half-page story describing the attacks on Wilson's candidacy by the social set who never forgave him for insisting on equality in college life. Ironically, the school later adopted a plan quite similar to the Quad Plan that is still in use today. Wilson would win the White House just two years after he left Princeton, and historians believe that it was this courageous fight over the inequities of the elitist club system that helped establish Wilson's reputation with the outside world as a champion of the underdog.

When Hobey entered the university, its country club

culture and elitist reputation were intact, and seventy-five percent of his class still hailed from private schools. The majority of the incoming student body, 325 in the class of 1914, recognized that they were part of a privileged American aristocracy and eagerly anticipated spending four years at Old Nassau. An exception was freshman Eugene O'Neill, who entered Princeton four years before Hobey in the class of 1910. As far as the future Nobel poet laureate was concerned, Princeton's life of athletics, compulsory chapel attendance and scholarship was not for him. He spent most of his first and only Princeton year in seedy Trenton bars, burlesque theaters, and whorehouses, and after a few bouts with the administration decided to quit before he was asked to leave. He later, however, succumbed to the mystique of Princeton and was quoted as saying that although he later spent some time at Harvard, his loyalty would always belong to Mother Princeton. Similarly, another Princeton student who failed to graduate, F. Scott Fitzgerald, would cherish his Princeton association throughout his entire life. His biographer, Andrew Turnbull, wrote of Fitzgerald's love affair with the university, "He thrilled to the poetry of Princeton – to the colorful crowds at the football games, to the snatches of song drifting across the campus, to the mellow lamplight back of Nassau Hall, to the whisperings in the pass at night in front of Witherspoon." Unfortunately for Scott, his love affair with the university did not extend to academics. He spent his entire freshman year writing an opera for his beloved Triangle Club. "To do this," he later recalled, "I failed algebra, trigonometry, co-ordinate geometry, and hygiene." No matter, for he worked with tutors during the summer and returned the following year to play the part of a chorus girl in his play.

Hobey Baker and six of his St. Paul's classmates roomed together for all four of their Princeton years above a restaurant on Nassau Street, in an apartment that they affectionately named "the Sweet Pea" after their beloved prep school. Hobey's reputation as a superb athlete had

spread to Princeton before he ever set foot on the campus. Those who did not know of him soon realized that
he was something special. A junior during Hobey's freshman year remembered his first encounter with the future
star. He and a few of his friends were playing an informal
game of hockey on Carnegie Lake, an artificial lake built
for crew with funds donated by Andrew Carnegie. The older students had just chosen sides when a boy approached
whom none of them recognized. Hobey Baker asked if he
could play in the game and joined the team that was playing against the juniors' squad. The older boy remembered
that once Hobey got hold of the puck, it was the last any of
them saw of it until he had skillfully buried it in their net.
He was a non-stop scoring machine, and one of his opponents on that cold New Jersey afternoon commented years
later that he had never, as a student or adult, seen a faster
skater. Hobey's reputation as a gentleman sportsman began
to take shape as he seemed almost apologetic, each time he
would strip another player of the puck and disappear down
the frozen pond. His position of local idol among the area's
prep school boys also took form that year. One contemporary recalled how Hobey would occasionally appear when
the local Lawrenceville boys would play a game of afternoon hockey on the area ponds. He remembered over fifty
years later how Hobey had fun with the boys, never showed
off and relished the role of teacher. He added that because
of those memorable pond games, the younger boys hero-
worshipped Baker years before he achieved national fame.
His skill on the ice was such that a semi-pro hockey team in
New York City invited him to play with their club during his
freshman year at Princeton. To his dismay, the university
forbid him from accepting the offer.

The freshman term at Princeton in the early twentieth century was still steeped in traditions designed to keep
the former prep school upperclassmen and "big men" in
their place. A nine o'clock curfew was strictly enforced until Washington's Birthday and freshmen were forbidden to

smoke pipes or cigars in public. Playing ball on the campus grounds was reserved for upperclassmen, and the new boys were expected to haul the lumber for the monstrous bonfires during athletic celebrations.

As far as dress was concerned, a freshman could not wear the school colors in any form. He was expected to wear cuffless trousers, a stiff collar, black tie, garters and the black skullcap known as a dink or beanie.

The university believed that the democratizing effect of the freshman dress code made it impossible to distinguish between the school athletic star or classroom idol and "the struggling minister's son who never got his name in the paper." While violent hazing was prohibited, the incoming class was expected to take part in organized "rushes" where the entire freshman class would storm the sophomores defending the university gym or cannon. Hobey may have been spared this ritual. William H. Edwards, a Princeton football captain at the turn of the century, would later write, "...shortly after college opens there must be a rush about the cannon...on that night in my freshman year great care was taken by Captain Cochran that none of the incoming football material engaged in the rush..." Rushing was later prohibited when a freshman was trampled to death during Fitzgerald's junior year.

"Horsing," a relic of more violent hazing, was another fading tradition that still existed, though in a less physical form, during Hobey's freshman term. There were formal horsing rules established by the omnipotent Senior Council in an effort to prevent injuries. Activities could not officially take place until one hour after the university opened in the autumn, and they were to take place for only ten days. Horsing was forbidden off campus, especially in front of the chapel and the platform of the railroad station. Described in the *American College University Series on Princeton* in 1914 as "noisy, amusing, always good natured," it was no doubt more amusing for the upperclassmen and observers than the horsing target. The boys were urged in the vernacular of the era to "hit it up" or entertain upperclassmen with a song or dance on their way to class and were often asked to march the "lockstep express" throughout the campus. A boy wearing a checkered jacket might be asked to remove it so his tormentors could play an impromptu game of checkers.

Hobey took the horsing and sophomore taunts in good spirit and vowed to be more charitable when it was his turn. A freshman during Baker's sophomore term remembered a nasty group of "horses' asses" from Hobey's class who gave him a particularly bad time. In contrast he recalled Baker as a friendly, courteous boy, dressed in his stylish, box-pleated gray Norfolk jacket and white flannels, who was always the gentleman and never took advantage of the defenseless freshmen.

As a freshman, Hobey quickly gained esteem on the football squad and everyone who watched him play knew he was the coming attraction. He was described by his classmates as a blond Adonis. One Princetonian who watched Hobey play in an era when men were not embarrassed to refer to another man as handsome or attractive described him as the most handsome boy he had ever seen. The university had no freshman hockey team so Hobey decided to play football as a left halfback. He weighed only 160 pounds and was just over five foot nine inches tall. Baker was lean, powerful and possessed the agility and speed of a tiger. He immediately caught the interest of the student body when he vaulted the freshman team to its first victory over Yale in years. In the style that would eventually make him a household name, he artfully faked a dropkick field goal attempt and ran twenty yards for a touchdown. Able to run the 100 yard dash in ten seconds, he proved so quick on the field that he would have to intentionally slow down on occasion in order not to overrun his own blockers. Baker never wore a helmet, and since players did not wear numbers on their jerseys during his era, Hobey's long blond hair quickly became his trademark. A spectator recalled years later that he was awestruck at how Baker "did everything with no apparent effort."

He played freshman baseball and was asked to join the swimming team when the coach spotted him in the pool and asked Hobey if he could time him swimming a few laps. A fellow member of the class of 1914 freshman team remembered that Hobey appeared to know little about baseball when practice began but was uncannily able to correct any error after being shown the correct way "only once." He was convinced that had Hobey chosen baseball as a varsity sport he could have been a star on the team. The same undergraduate recalled how Hobey was diving off the springboard like an expert a half-hour after receiving, "a little coaching." His athletic ability never ceased to amaze his fellow students. The university rifle team was conducting tryouts for the team and some of the school's best shots were attempting to qualify. Hobey wandered into the range with no shooting experience and no particular desire to make the team. After an afternoon of abbreviated instruction, the golden boy had the crack shots shaking their heads as he effortlessly recorded a score that qualified him for the team.

Although there was no freshman hockey team, Hobey would stay in shape on the local ponds or wherever he could pick up a game. In February of 1911, he agreed to travel to Poughkeepsie, New York to play an informal game against a local team. He and his friends were looking forward to the contest since it was to be played on a small, natural lake near Vassar College and they would have an opportunity to skate with the college girls after the game. It must have been quite a sight because the local undertaker had provided a couple of limousines to transport the teams to the ice. As the boys rode to the lake, one of the local stars mentioned that he had read that a star hockey player had just entered Princeton and that he hoped they hadn't brought him along. They all had a good laugh when it was pointed out to him that he was sitting next to Hobey in the limousine. Unfortunately, the ice was so soft that it was almost unplayable, but since the boys did not want to disappoint the local crowd and especially the Vassar girls, they played one period. The short contest ended in a 1-1 tie with Hobey scoring a goal. Sadly, Sam Crump, the good-natured local boy who had sat next to Hobey in the limousine that day, would, like Hobey, never return from the war in Europe. But on that crisp winter day, there was the game and the pretty Vassar girls, and as the young men boarded the train for Princeton, all was right with the world.

Hobey also excelled at football during his days at St. Paul's. The rising star is in the middle row, fourth from the left, of this vintage image of the 1909 football squad.

"Football....there's murder in that game..."
John L. Sullivan - heavyweight champion
(1882-1892)

Chapter Three

The first inter-collegiate football game in the United States was played between Rutgers and Princeton on November 6, 1869, when a contingency of Princeton men traveled to New Brunswick, New Jersey to accept a Rutgers challenge. A small crowd gathered on that blustery autumn day to unknowingly witness an historic contest that in reality resembled a soccer match more than the football game we know today. The students, dressed in street clothes, attempted to score goals by driving a small, round ball through primitive goal posts set approximately twenty-five feet apart. This could be achieved by kicking or hand-batting airborne balls, but any kind of throwing or passing was prohibited. The rules were simple: the first team to score six goals was the winner. Rutgers won by a score of 6-4. Although various forms of football had been played decades earlier by eastern college undergraduates, often as part of hazing rituals, most historians recognize this contest played by fifty students on the Rutgers commons to be the beginning of collegiate football.

Three decades later, Helen Keller, a student at Radcliffe in 1899, confirmed just how popular the fledgling sport had grown when she described the annual 1899 Harvard-Yale game. The blind and deaf undergraduate wrote of feeling the ground rumble from the bedlam at the stadium located blocks from her room. She recalled "hearing" the cheering of the 25,000 spectators as clearly as if they had been in her room and compared the tumult to "the din of war and not of a football game."

Another contemporary report described the standing room only Harvard-Yale game of 1900 and how in an effort to accommodate the numerous fans that could not obtain tickets, the Knickerbocker Club in Manhattan arranged a play-by-play account of the game live via telegraph.

The three decades between the first soccer-like football game and "The Game," as the annual Harvard-Yale contest that Helen Keller described became known, produced a uniquely American sport that the dynamic Baker would soon dominate. Not too long after the first intercollegiate game in 1869, more than twenty years before Hobey was born, the eastern colleges began an on-again, off-again love affair with football. University presidents and faculty questioned whether athletics had any place on campus, but the proponents of Christian manhood prevailed. Princeton and Rutgers continued to issue challenges to each other and eventually Columbia, Yale and Harvard were drawn into competition. Harvard played a hand in the further development of the game by adopting a style of play called the Boston game. This improvement to the soccer-like game resembled rugby and permitted the players to run with the ball, throw it and tackle each other. Harvard refused to compete in the newly organized Intercollegiate Football Association unless its style of play was adopted. The boys eventually got together and to this day Harvard historians believe that the origin of the modern game was a match played between Harvard and Montreal's McGill University in May of 1874 and not the 1869 Princeton-Rutgers game. They have a strong point since the modern game resembles their Boston game more than the New Brunswick affair.

Representatives from four universities – Harvard, Yale, Princeton, and Columbia – later got together at Springfield, Massachusetts on November 26, 1876 to form a new Intercollegiate Football Association and adopted the rugby style of play. This was the origin of the term Ivy League or IV league, named not for the climbing, shiny-leafed evergreen shrub that adorns their venerable campus structures, but for the simple Roman numeral for the number four, IV.

In 1880 new rules established more of the modern game we know today. The team complement was set at eleven men, and more importantly the game was further differentiated from its parent, rugby, by the introduction of the scrimmage. No longer would there be continuous play dictated by the unpredictable rugby scrum, but a snap of the ball would begin play, and there would be a pause in the action when a player was brought down.

Unfortunately, it became apparent that football was developing into an extremely dangerous game. When asked to comment on the state of collegiate football at the close of the nineteenth century, heavyweight champion John L. Sullivan remarked, "There's murder in that game." He noted that in prizefighting, both men understood their task and went about their business, one on one, face to face. The goal was simple and direct...inflict as much harm on your opponent as possible. He then went on to say that in football, "There's eleven guys trying to do you in." Here was the Boston Strong Boy, a man who fought with his bare knuckles for a living, describing a college boy's game as brutal and dangerous. While his remarks may seem far- fetched, the truth was that the unique game of American football had developed into a deadly pastime. In 1905, eighteen people lost their lives playing football. The mortality rate leveled off for a few years and then hit a high of forty-two in 1909, the year before Hobey Baker enrolled at Princeton. Boys were dying from body blows, spinal injuries and concussions. No wonder it was reported that in 1879, noted artist

Frederic Remington, a devoted football player during his student days at Yale, dipped his football jersey in blood at a local slaughterhouse before a Yale-Princeton game. When asked why he did it, he replied, "To make it look more business like." A sports writer went as far as to speculate on whether biting had any place in the game of football.

Football became lethal because it was a work in progress. There were no blueprints for the hybrid game, and as each new rule was introduced, another one was required to stop some tactic that the former rule had inadvertently permitted. For example in 1888, rule changes designed to "open up" the game and make it faster, legalized tackling below the waist and blocking in front of the ball runner. Instead of opening the game, the rule changes had the opposite effect. Teams realized that even their swiftest runner had difficulty gaining significant yardage against the new legalized below the waist tackling rule. They responded by contracting their offensive line shoulder to shoulder near the ball, pulling their backs in close to the line with the idea of pushing and pulling the ball carrier through the defensive line in a mass play. The engine that drove the brutal mass play was the rule that allowed the players to go into motion before the ball was snapped. The backs charged forward en masse before the ball was in play which created the one-half ton, bone-crushing momentum in the mass play that ran over the opponent's defensive line. The results were more broken bones and crushed heads as variations of mass plays were created, such as Harvard's infamous flying wedge and Princeton's deadly V wedge. Columbia introduced a play called the hurdle. In this murderous play, one of their smallest players would receive the ball about five yards behind their compacted front line, get up a good head of steam and literally use the back of the center to springboard himself into orbit. If the opposing team pushed him back, his own team would push him forward. Not to be outdone, a Princeton mastermind designed the anti-hurdle play and launched one of their men at the same time the Columbia player lunged forward. They collided in midair and were carried off the field in pieces. Quick, wiry, compact athletes took a back seat to the titans needed to provide the sheer force required to break through their opponent's line. The strategy was primitive; fearless, young, iron men would pound away until something gave. More often than not, it was a spine or skull that caved before the line would break. Initially, reporters characterized the new mass play strategy as Napoleonic tactics, triumphantly smashing the enemy's weakest defensive point, but later called for an end to them as violent and boring. Crowds were horrified at the carnage created when the unprotected players converged around their ball carrier to form a human wedge that was supposed to shield the carrier while slamming into their opponent's defensive line.

More cries came for the abolishment of the game, and after a particularly bloody Harvard-Yale game in 1894, dubbed by the press as the Hampden Park Blood Bath, the two schools cancelled "The Game" for two years. One foreign correspondent filed a report on that memorable game in Hampden Park stating, "..it turned into an awful butchery." Most attempts to permanently abolish football were thwarted because the popular press of the day discovered that the infant sport sold newspapers and the crowds continued to grow.

How an insignificant college game, enjoyed primarily by the players and a small base of spectators from the three elite eastern universities, grew to a major sporting event that could fill 50,000 and 78,000 capacity stadiums can be attributed to two people, William Randolph Hearst and Joseph Pulitzer. Both men and their newspapers, Hearst's *New York Journal* and Pulitzer's *New York World,* in an effort to build their circulation and outdo each other, created the modern newspaper that we know today. Each man introduced innovation after innovation in order to stay ahead of the pack of the over fifty-five daily newspapers that existed in New York City at the close of the nineteenth century. Pulitzer pressured Hearst by introducing illustrations as a rule rather than an exception and by creating a first-class sports section. Hearst responded with his own innovations, and the public began to expect entertainment as well as news in the daily newspaper. Collegiate football reaped the benefits of this competition and helped fill the void created when the professional baseball season ended in the fall. Football gained popularity with the introduction of the Thanksgiving Day Championship Game, played off campus in the New York area at places like the old Polo Grounds or Manhattan Field. The exciting autumn contest pitted the eastern college champions in games that eventually became a social event, officially launching the winter holiday season. A parade took place up Fifth Avenue with carriages decorated in Yale blue or Princeton orange and black, and everyone, from a bank clerk to a debutante, was an alumnus on that day. A young boy who was inadvertently caught in the festivities before the 1891 Yale-Princeton game played at the Polo Grounds later wrote of the impact the event had on him. "The whole scene was intensely thrilling to me, and I did not leave until the last player entered the carriage and left for the field." He further recalled, "I watched them with indescribable fascination. It stirred something within me, and down deep in my soul there was born a desire to go to college." By the time this boy witnessed the parade and game, Pulitzer and Hearst had created such intense interest in the collegiate game that forty to fifty thousand fans from all classes of society attended the Thanksgiving Game. Hundreds of thousands of new fans who could not attend the game anxiously awaited the latest edition of their daily paper to read about their college hero and see the marvelous illustrations. The New York area Thanksgiving Day Championship Games took place for only a brief period of time, and by 1896, with pressure mounting to prevent another Hampden Park Blood Bath, the college administrators decided for "moral reasons" to play their intercollegiate games either on or near their own campuses. But by then, the genie was out of the bottle. If the games did not come to the city, the city would descend on the campuses. The newspaper continued to report on the games wherever they were played, and the railroads were forced to put special trains in service on game day. In response, the universities constructed massive arenas to accommodate the spectators and reap the financial benefits.

The publishers could have chosen to focus on other college sports, but they realized that football touched a nerve in the restless American urban male. Office workers discovered that the physical qualities required to open the Western frontier or fight heroically in the Civil War were not required in the industrial modern culture. Brute strength, once a key to survival, was now superfluous for the modern man. The word *masculine* was no longer only used to designate traits that distinguished men from women. It now took on a more judgmental definition; if a man was not masculine or "manly," then he could be considered womanly. No sport conjured up the new ideal of masculinity more than college football.

In the fall of 1905, in an effort to reform football and prevent more deaths, President Theodore Roosevelt summoned the football powers from the Big Three – Harvard, Princeton, and Yale – along with Yale's Walter Camp, the father of American football, to Washington to discuss the state of the game. Roosevelt's love for the game and the strenuous life prompted the meeting, but another motive was that his eldest son, Ted, might play football for the Harvard freshman team. His diminutive stature, 5'7" and less than 150 pounds, would prevent him from playing with the varsity squad, but nonetheless neither Roosevelt nor his wife, wanted to see their child injured. How important was the problem and how important had the game become in the public's eyes? *The New York Times* applauded Roosevelt for his initiative on a "question of vital interest to the American people..." The president asked the group to draft a statement that condemned brutality, supported fair play and adherence to the rules. They obeyed the commander-in-chief, but the injuries continued. While many educators, including Harvard's powerful, outspoken president, Charles Eliot, wished to abolish the sport, the majority believed that reform, not abolition, was the answer. Eliot maligned the sport in his report to the Board of Overseers for the 1904-05 academic year. He wrote that "the American game of football as now played is unfit for colleges and schools....As a spectator spectacle football is more brutalizing than prize-fighting, cock-fighting or bull fighting..." Cooler heads prevailed. New rules and President Roosevelt's intervention saved the game.

By the time Hobey Baker began his Princeton football career, the national stage had been set for the college football hero, and someone with Hobey's athletic ability and movie star looks was just what the public hungered for. The year that Baker enrolled, 1910, also marked the end of the vicious, deadly mass plays in football. The ever evolving game and its very active rules committee had in 1910 enacted new rules that moved the games closer to the sport that we know today. The forward pass, long detested by football purists and hampered by rules that restricted its use, was now to become part of the game in an effort to open up the play, reduce injuries, and please the spectators. The mass plays, such as the flying wedge or V wedge disappeared with a new rule that prohibited the linemen from lining up in the backfield on offense. The pushing and pulling of the ball carrier along with interlocked interference was also prohibited in an effort to prevent the catastrophic injuries that had accompanied the horrific collisions of muscle and bone. In addition, the game was divided into fifteen-minute quarters instead of twenty-minute quarters.

The new rules that outlawed mass play increased the value of agile, fleet-footed players like Hobey Baker. His football career would have been limited or perhaps nonexistent had he been forced to compete during the mass play era. He only weighed 160 pounds when he played for

Princeton. The new rules also greatly reduced serious injuries, and in 1912, the rules committee promoted the forward pass and increased scoring by voting to eliminate the remaining pass restrictions and adding a fourth down to gain ten yards. This key change provided the quarterback with a chance to pass before he had to kick. The committee also reduced the size of the ball to accommodate the forward pass.

Although the college rules committee had approved the forward pass in an effort to open up the game, the eastern universities were slow to embrace the pass. Old habits die hard, and the old grads encouraged their younger brethren to play the game the way they believed it should be played. Princeton had no resident full-time coach as it was considered poor form to employ a professional. The tradition was for gridiron stars of the previous year's team to coach the current one. This perpetuated the old style of play and left little room for experimentation in passing or strategy. Editorials in the university newspaper cried out for the open game, but the alum coaches stuck to the traditional ways. The new rules had eliminated the brutal mass plays, and the college football death toll fell below five. Most of the eastern players were so uncomfortable with passing the cumbersome ball that the game developed into kicking duels where a team's goal was to get rid of the ball, gain field advantage and hope to capitalize on a fumble or blocked punt. Defense and opportunism ruled the day. It was not unusual for a game to be decided by a field goal or to end in a scoreless tie like the 1910 and 1911 Harvard-Yale games.

Hobey's skill as a freshman player was rewarded when he made the 1911 varsity team. He began his football career in the midst of an ultra defensive style era where a drop-kick field goal was scored more than the touchdown. The most important players on a team during this period were a safety-man with good hands and a deadly drop-kicker. Hobey Baker was both, and his talents were uniquely suited for this style of football. While the drop kick is still legal

today in the NFL, it has not been attempted in a game for
over sixty years because its effectiveness has been negated
by the tapered shape of the pigskin design. The ball used
today is thinner and more oblong than the rounder style
ball used during Hobey's day. In the early days of the game
a skilled drop-kicker would time the drop perfectly and
kick the ball just as it touched the ground.

This was also the era of the "preliminary season"
when Harvard, Princeton and Yale would play their weaker
sisters in the league before facing each other for the big
games in November. After seven early season "tune-up" victories over Rutgers (37-0) and Colgate (31-0) and others,
Hobey and the undefeated Tigers played a Harvard team
that was considered the best in the country and won the
contest 8-6 before a crowd of twenty-two thousand at Princeton's University Field.

The crown jewel of the season was a memorable
game played on a muddy Yale Field where Old Nassau defeated the Eli's big blue juggernaut for the first time in eight
years. Yale's Art Howe kicked a field goal to put the New
Haven boys ahead, but Princeton's Sam White later capi-
talized on a Yale fumble, recovered the slippery ball and
ran sixty-eight yards for a touchdown. In the defensive style
of play of the era, Princeton achieved the 6-3 victory over
Yale without making a first down. Hobey caught the eye of
the press and the fans by not dropping a single punt. The
newspapers reported that his expert handling of the wet,
slippery ball helped save the day for Princeton. The Tigers
won eight games and lost none during Hobey's first year
on the varsity squad and were crowned the 1911 national
champions by the eastern press. The team was honored at
a ceremony held at the Philadelphia Princeton Club where
each member was presented with inscribed gold cuff links.
As part of the memorable ceremony, Hobey's father, "Bobby," a gridiron star for the Tigers in 1883, joined his son at
the podium.

The game had reached its fifth decade, and the ritu-

als surrounding the contests had become cherished traditions. The excitement of a big game could transform a small
village into a bustling metropolis as forty thousand fans or
more would arrive for the tilt. The major New York newspapers would devote three or four pages out of an eight
page Sunday supplement to a major eastern college game.
Everyone was a cheerleader as the Yale faithful would rock
the bleachers with sophomore Cole Porter's "Bull Dog."

> *Bull Dog! Bull Dog!*
> *Bow wow wow!*
> *Eli Yale!*
> *Bull Dog! Bull Dog!*
> *Bow wow wow!*
> *Our team can never fail.*

Porter had caught the student body's attention in
1910 when he won a student competition for a new football fight song. His "Bingo, Eli Yale" was an instant hit with
uncomplicated, memorable lines such as "Bingo! Bingo!,
That's the Lingo" and was published by a noted New York
City sheet music company. Porter won the contest the following year with "Bull Dog," and his musical career was off
and running. He would eventually write over 300 songs
while a student at Yale. The diminutive songwriter also
penned six full-scale musical productions for the university,
many with a central theme of the superiority and sexual
prowess of the Yale man.

Not to be outdone, the Orange and Black tiger fans
had their wordsmith. F. Scott Fitzgerald's award-winning,
"A Cheer for Princeton," was a favorite among the sons of
Old Nassau. The pen that would someday give the world
The Great Gatsby and *This Side of Paradise* thrilled the Tigers
with catchy phrases like:

> *Princeton, cheer for Princeton,*

Raise your voices, loud and free
Strong and steady
Ever ready
For defeat or victory.

Harvard's John Reed, who would later achieve fame with his firsthand account of the Russian Revolution, *Ten Days That Shook the World,* was a rabid fan and cheerleader who would unabashedly exhort the crimson crowd to destroy the hated Elis or Tigers.

Hobey joined the freshman football team at Princeton in 1910 and immediately caught the eye of the student body. He vaulted the team to its first victory over Yale in years when he faked a drop-kick and ran twenty yards for a touchdown. His skill and sportsmanship were rewarded when he was placed on the varsity squad in his sophomore year. Hobey is seated third from the left.

"The team that won't be beat, can't be beat."

John Prentiss Poe Jr., Princeton - Class of 1895

Chapter Four

Legend states that in 1916, just before the Elis were to take the field, Yale coach, Tad Jones, fired up his team by reminding the nineteen and twenty-year-old boys that they were going out to play Harvard and that " ....never again in your whole life will you do anything so important." This was the atmosphere that surrounded Ivy League football during Hobey Baker's career, and although hockey was his first love, his gridiron talents were recognized by the press and the public and feared by Princeton's opponents. In the defensive era that he played in, three of the most valued skills on the field were punt receiving, field goal kicking and open field running. Hobey could do all three superbly, and as a safety-man and drop-kicker, he supplied the drama that filled the coliseum-like stadiums that were rising to accommodate the modern day gladiators and their fans. Harvard Stadium opened in 1903 and could accommodate 40,000 fans. It was later enlarged to seat 50,000 people. Many of the spectators who witnessed the sure-handed Baker receive a punt remembered his charismatic performances almost sixty years after his death. It did not harm Hobey's image that he was easy on the eyes.

A contemporary wrote of Hobey, "In my opinion, I have seldom seen a more charming, attractive and handsome boy." Hobey electrified the crowds with his reckless, uncanny ability to judge the spot on a kick where the ball would land, catch it on the run and break down the field as the opponent's ends converged on him. Unlike today, tacklers were not required to wait for the kick to start before they began running downfield. This made Hobey a target, and reports abound of the savage treatment he received game after game. *The New York Times* reported on a game where Hobey received "shocks enough to put the ordinary player out of commission, yet he came up always smiling and never hurt." His legend grew as the press reported that his, "returns of punts excited universal comment." He would often gain more yards during a game on his punt returns than both teams did from scrimmage. The crowds would rise to their feet when a punt formation was called for they knew they were about to see something special. A fellow student recalled Hobey "waiting tensely, moving his feet up and down, and watching the ball." He went on to remember, "When Hobey caught it on the run…he was gone and gave the onlookers heart failure." Another student noted that this was in the era when "…a punt touching the ground put all of the kickers side 'on side' and made the ball eligible for recovery by them….in other words, a punt just had to be caught." All who witnessed Hobey grab a punt out of mid-air while storming down the field agreed that he had no equal. His legend grew. P.D Haughton, the Harvard coach during Baker's career, described Hobey as very fast and praised him as a naturally expert end runner. He went on to say that Hobey was out there like a streak and always looked for the "big opening." Another Princeton undergraduate remembered how the girls would slow down to get a glimpse of the portrait of Hobey that was displayed in the window of a popular photography studio on Nassau Street. "Hobey, as I recall, was not only the athletic hero, but the idol, the positive influence for good, on innumerable people," he added. No wonder that in a letter written in 1963, a seventy-year-old man who witnessed Baker play in his youth, remembered that Hobey, "looked pretty much the way I suppose Greek gods looked." A New York sportswriter advised spectators who were new to the game to, "just watch his blond head, those of you who don't quite grasp the finer points of the game, and you won't miss a play, for 'Hobey' is wherever the ball is."

Hobey routinely dazzled both his fans and opponents when he would break free for one of his patented open field runs. *The Boston Herald* wrote in 1912, "Hobey Baker is the most feared open field runner now playing the game of football. Let him get free and clear with the ball tucked under his arm, and it is good night to his pursuers..." He established his credentials as one of the most talented runners in the game in a contest against Dartmouth in his junior year when he caught a punt on Princeton's 15-yard line and ran the remaining 85 yards for a touchdown. A *New York Times* reporter noted that "the entire Dartmouth team was between (Hobey) and a touchdown when he started but he dodged one, threw off another, sprinted beyond the next one, and finally escaped the entire team." The headlines read, "Tigers Devour Big Dartmouth," and the sportswriters began to refer to Hobart Amory Hare Baker as just plain *Hobey*. His fans would eagerly await the next edition of their local paper to see what Hobey was up to. The media noted that New Jersey Governor and presidential candidate Woodrow Wilson was in attendance to witness Baker's magic during the Dartmouth contest. The New York press referred to Baker as the "artful dodger," zigzagging his way toward the goal line and added that the crowd favorite never failed to come up smiling and seemingly unharmed after being repeatedly and savagely thrown to the ground. They wrote that "Baker has about the shiftiest pair of feet and the speediest hands and eyes as you will find attached to anyone." Hobey's crowd-pleasing, punt-receiving trademark would often put him in harm's way as his reputation grew, and frustrated opponents threw everything they had at the 160 pound Tiger, the lightest starter on the Princeton team. "Get Baker," proclaimed the headline of a Manhattan newspaper, informing the horrified reader that the word had been passed down the line of future opponents to stop the wonder boy, whatever way necessary, or face defeat. During the same Dartmouth game in which Hobey scored the 85-yard touchdown, he caught a weak punt and realizing that he was in field goal position called for a free catch. The Dartmouth players disregarded Baker's signal and viciously crushed him. Baker picked himself off the field, moved fifteen yards closer to the goal posts thanks to the Dartmouth penalty, and easily booted the ball over the crossbar to fire up the Old Nassau faithful. He seemed impervious to pain.

The second weapon in the Baker arsenal was his skill at drop-kicking, and Hobey was second only to Harvard's famous kicker, Charles Brickley. In games that were often decided without a touchdown, the field goal took on added significance. In his junior year, Hobey kicked a pair of field goals that gave the Tigers a 6-6 tie against mighty Yale. The rivalry between the Yale Bulldogs and the Princeton Tigers was second only to the Harvard-Yale tradition. In Hobey's senior year, the Princeton football eleven took on the mighty Bulldogs before 35,000 spectators in New Haven. The weather was perfect for football, and a chill in the air sent scores of pretty women running for their finest furs. From early morning until game time, the crowds poured into town. Seventeen special football trains were required to transport over 20,000 fans from New York City. *The New York Times* called it "the greatest gathering that ever witnessed a Princeton game." The day was historic, the last Princeton-Yale played on the old Yale Field gridiron. The big games were being moved the following season to the brand-new, coliseum-like, Yale Bowl. There was a festive mood throughout the city with almost every woman sporting either a white chrysanthemum for Yale or a yellow one for Princeton. The newspapers would later comment on the other contest that was taking place: the fashion show of hundreds and hundreds of debutantes mingling through the colorful crowd vying for the gentlemen's attention. Many agreed that the girl who received the most admiration was an exceptionally pretty young Princeton supporter who wore a velvet gown of bright orange trimmed with black fur. Street vendors sold tin bulldogs and tigers, and it seemed like every person in town had his own college flag or pennant.

The restaurants had prepared for the hungry crowds and all were accommodated. One enterprising and partisan shopkeeper displayed in his window a realistic looking Bengal tiger being roasted over a fiery gridiron by a Yale chef. Quite the crowd pleaser, the hapless tiger wiggled its tail, rolled its eyes and opened its mouth as it was being roasted.

Princeton had been favored to win, but as the game began, the Yale fans were pleased to see that the teams seemed evenly matched. The time seemed appropriate to serenade the hometown crowd with their new song, "Good Night, Princeton." The partisan fans sang out:

Good night, poor Princeton,
You're tucked in tight.
When the big blue team
Gets after you,
Princeton, good night

It began to look like a bad afternoon for Old Nassau as Guernsey of Yale scored first, kicking the ball over the crossbar for a field goal. This turn of events prompted the Eli fans to break into their favorite class chant:

Oh, more work for the undertaker
Another little job for the casket maker

A newspaper later noted that a blaze of shimmering

blue waved over the Yale stands after that field goal, and cheers rang out like a series of cannon shots for over five minutes. The Princeton faithful would not be deterred and answered the Eli congregation with a lively rendition of "Going Back to Nassau Hall." Predictions of a wide-open game proved inaccurate as a brutal contest developed, Yale protecting the narrow lead and neither team wanting to make a mistake. *The New York Times* reported that it was, " a bruising, desperately fought game," and went on to remind their readers that "football of this kind is a man's work ...no pastime for the faint hearts."

Hobey tried in vain to break through the huge blue line, and time and again was viciously smashed to the ground. Rather than achieve the victory that was predicted by the experts, Princeton now hoped for a miracle to prevent an embarrassing defeat.

As fate would permit, it was Hobey who spoiled the Yale victory and saved his team's honor. As the thousands of spectators watched in amazement, all realized that a forty-three-yard Princeton field goal attempt by Baker was all that stood between a Yale victory and humiliation for Old Nassau.

Hobey wiped the perspiration from his forehead and prepared to kick the forty-plus yard field goal. A reporter for the *Times* noted that "(e)ven Princeton men whispered: 'he will never do it'." Thousands of Yale fans screamed for one of the Eli eleven to break through and block the kick. Hobey dropped back and his fearless demeanor immediately quieted the 35,000 spectators now on their feet. Every eye was on Hobey as he received the pass, dropped it to his toe, and gracefully sent the ball over the crossbars.

He not only kicked the equalizer but would preserve the tie when late in the game a Yale halfback, Ainsworth, broke through the entire Tiger team and ran eighty-four yards before Hobey brought him down with a flying tackle on the Princeton six-yard line. *The New York Times* described the fantastic rush:

" One by one he passed the Princeton tacklers. Three different men hurled themselves at Ainsworth and he scampered by them all. The rabid crowd, fired to a point of frenzy, howled for a touchdown. Ainsworth was now clear of everybody but Hobey Baker, playing far back toward the Princeton goal. The Princeton captain alone could save Princeton now. "

Baker held his ground and did not commit until he was sure which way the speedy halfback would run. It was a cat and mouse game, and at the last possible second Hobey hurled himself at Ainsworth. The Yale crowd let out a collective groan, as the airborne Tiger captain pulled their hero down on the Princeton six-yard line. The big blue line now had four attempts to carry or pass the ball over the line, and although the Princeton line bent, it did not break, and the game ended in a 3-3 tie. Hobey Baker had saved the day for Old Nassau.

No wonder lifetime Tiger football enthusiast, F. Scott Fitzgerald, once described Baker as "an ideal worthy of everything in my enthusiastic admiration, yet consummated and expressed in a human being who stood within ten feet of me."

On November 13th of his senior year Hobey was awarded the Princeton varisty letter for football. He was the school leader, having been awarded the letter the largest number of times, five times for football and three times for hockey. This was the most anyone could possibly win under the two major sport rules at Princeton at that time. He had been unanimously selected to captain the team in his senior year, and during his watch Princeton never lost to Yale. Hobey caught over nine hundred punts in his three varsity seasons and averaged three hundred yards per game on punt returns alone. The 92 points he scored in football in 1912 stood as an individual Princeton season scoring record for sixty years. His three-year record of 180 points stood until 1964. Another Princeton All-American, Cosmo Iacavazzi, squeaked past Hobey's record in the final quarter of the last game of his college career. Baker fans like to remind the record-keepers that a few of Baker's touchdowns were scored in 1911 when they only counted for five points.

Hobey was an All-American in football twice at Princeton and is a member of the College Football Hall of Fame.

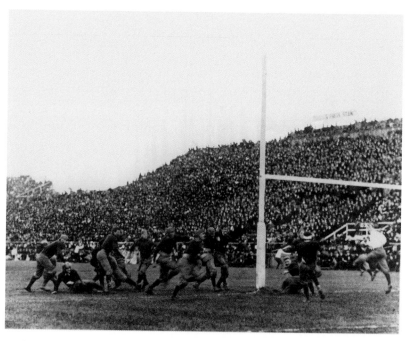

Princeton vs. Yale in 1913. Hobey Baker saved the Tigers from certain defeat when he kicked a 43-yard field goal. He then preserved the hard fought tie when he tackled the Yale halfback at the Princeton six-yard line. The golden boy can be seen in this image blocking at the right.

"Passion for fame; a passion which is the instinct of all great souls..."

Edmund Burke

Chapter Five

Hobey may have played football in a conservative, defensive-minded, low-scoring period of the game's history, but he was blessed to play collegiate hockey just as the fast-moving sport was hitting its stride. A primitive form of hockey had been played at Princeton since the 1890's, and as the game evolved, the university along with Harvard, Yale, Dartmouth and Columbia formed the Intercollegiate Hockey League in 1900. Hockey became recognized as an official sport of the University Athletic Association in 1904.

While Hobey Baker was busy gaining fame as a Princeton freshman football star, the press spent that year eagerly anticipating his first varsity hockey game. This was the era when New York City had a dozen daily newspapers, and more than a few editors prayed that the buzz about Hobey was true. Never known to disappoint his fans or the press, Hobey gave them an inaugural show that set the bar for the rest of his career on ice. Lacking indoor rinks of their own at the time, the Ivy League teams would often play their series in ice rinks in Boston, Philadelphia and New York. This provided a "big-time" venue that few college hockey teams experience today.

Hobey played when hockey was a seven-man affair and not a game for the meek at heart. Substitutions were permitted, but because a starter replaced by another player could not return in the same period, fearless players became adept at nursing or masking injuries in order to remain on the ice. The positions at that time were goal, point (defense), cover point (defense), left wing, center, right wing and rover. Six-man hockey was not officially adopted until 1922. In an era when the forward pass was illegal, Hobey's position, rover, was as the name implies, the free wheeling, primary, offensive and sometimes defensive player on the ice.

Baker's varsity debut took place against a formidable Williams College squad at the St. Nicholas Arena, located at 66th Street and Columbus Avenue in New York City. Princeton desperately needed to start the new season with a victory since the previous season had ended in an embarrassing tie for last place. Hobey became the darling of the New York press and Princeton University as he systematically dismantled the Williams' defense, scoring six goals and three assists before a sellout crowd in the 14-0 Princeton victory. Baker was everywhere on the ice and seemed to score at will from any angle. A schoolmate who watched the golden-haired sophomore effortlessly shake off the towering Williams defensemen wrote years later that from that point on he knew the meaning of beauty wedded to strength.

Hobey's celebrated abilities on the ice are even more extraordinary when framed in the context of the period. While some advances had been made in ice skates by the time Hobey played for Princeton, skate blades were still long, flat and thick and resembled modern day goalie skates. No one expected a player at that time to dance on the ice the way Hobey could. The skates made it difficult to turn quickly or change directions on the ice, and that along with the no-forward pass rule set the stage for an offense consisting mainly of straight line lateral rushes countered by straight line skating defensemen. To the amazement of the appreciative spectators, Hobey changed all that. He would skate through and around the hapless defensemen with the puck seemingly attached to the blade of his stick. A *New York Times* sportswriter described Baker curving and gliding through the field of skaters with a "daring and graceful ease" that made the other players appear to be sleepwalking. The opposition would slash and hack at Hobey in vain as he covered the distance of the rink with a few powerful strides.

The club-like hockey sticks were nothing like the puck launchers of today so the most valuable player on the ice was the skilled stick-handler who could carry the puck into the enemy's territory. Whether it was innate ability or the product of his years of practice as a young boy during the endless New England winters, Hobey could skate the puck without looking down at the ice. This was no small talent considering the condition of the ice in the pre-Zamboni era. There was no precise, automated cleaning and scraping of the ice, and after a few minutes of play the ruts and snow mounds would make quality stick handling and skating all but impossible.

A St.Paul's student who followed Baker's college career on the ice remembered years later that Hobey seemed to be able to stop at will without turning his skates sideways in the ninety-degree, traditional hockey stop and then effortlessly skate backwards. Baker stopped by turning in his toes, which permitted him to stop and change direction on a dime. Another contemporary of Baker's, a fellow Princeton graduate, wrote fifty years after Hobey's death that his skating was one of the most beautiful things he had ever had the privilege to see.

When Hobey played hockey, almost every spectator became indelibly imprinted with a special memory that many carried to their grave. Five decades after Baker laced up a pair of skates for the last time, a spectator wrote of Hobey's wizardry with the puck. He recalled how the puck seemed to be attached to Baker's stick by some invisible thread and added that he had never seen a human being move so fast under his own power. *"Ankles of steel...,"* *"my hero and idol...,"* *"...one of the most attractive natural athletes I have seen or known."* Had these spectator accolades not been so numerous and unanimous, it might seem that Hobey was a fictitious hero, created by an imaginative Hollywood scriptwriter.

Though memories fade and are sometimes embellished when recalling a favorite hero, unsentimental newspaper accounts of long-lost games are an accurate window to the past. In the case of Hobey Baker, these reports verify the cherished memories of those who witnessed his magic on the ice. In a Princeton varsity game played against Harvard at the St. Nicholas Rink in New York City, *The New York Times* reported that "Hobey cut loose at intervals and went through the Harvard team as if the Crimson players were standing still." The Harvard team's top defensemen smothered Baker, but as the excited reporter noted, they "could not prevent him from making his sensational sorties and feeding the puck to his mates." The Tigers won by a score of 4-1 with Hobey tallying three assists.

Another match against Harvard, played in the old Boston Arena, resulted in a 3-2 Princeton victory with Hobey scoring two goals. *The New York Times* headline proclaimed, "Brilliant Hockey by Baker Defeats Harvard in Boston Rink." As Baker skated the puck toward the Crimson goal, the deafening roar of the five thousand spectators forced the officials to throw away the whistles and resort to using hand signals to signal offside plays. So dominant was his play that newspaper reports began to describe the Tiger team as, "Hobey Baker and six other players."

By his senior year, Hobey had become a major celebrity in New York City and wherever the sport was played. No collegiate hockey player before or after Baker has ever achieved such fame. On February 1, 1914, *The New York Times* reported an account of an exciting game between the Princeton Tigers and the Yale team. The high-priced tickets were sold a week before the game so the St. Nicholas Rink was literally jammed to the rafters with Baker fans. The reporter proclaimed that "Baker is idolized more than any other player who ever played at the rink." Hobey grabbed the puck behind his own goal and skated it down the ice through the Yale defense at lightning speed. He zigzagged toward the opponent's goal as the Eli skaters hooked and slashed at him in vain. The anxious Yale goalie, realizing that he was the only thing between Baker and the goal, staked his claim in the crease and prepared to hold his ground. Applause thundered through the building as Hobey accelerated, entered the enemy's zone, and scored from a seemingly impossible angle. The newspaper account noted, "Hobey Baker has become the king of the ice in the eyes of New York hockey fans." Baker's touching the puck was an occasion for deafening cheers and shouts that "would flatter a conquering hero," exclaimed the sportswriter. The final 3-1 Princeton victory was secondary to the exiting fans. They had seen a living legend and would never forget the Tigers' golden boy. The headlines continued: "Hobey Baker Still Team in Himself on the Ice" or "Baker Stars as Usual."

As Hobey's fame grew, so did his reputation as a gentleman athlete. Princeton students were only permitted to play two varsity sports, and Hobey had decided on football and hockey, two very dangerous activities. The public and press marveled at the savagery that these upper class boys exhibited on both the gridiron and ice rink. These bluebloods took their hero Teddy Roosevelt's words to heart when he proclaimed, "Do not hit at all if it can be avoided, but never hit softly," and later added, "In life, as in a football game, the principle is: hit the line hard; don't foul and don't shirk, but hit the line hard."

"Don't foul." This was the law of the gentleman athlete or man of action who played hard for the love of sport. Winning was secondary to playing by the code, and losing a hard-fought contest was nothing to be ashamed of. In Hobey's era to be called a "mucker" (manure) meant that you were a poor sportsman who took unfair advantage of another player and brought shame upon yourself, your team and your school. A professional athlete was considered the worst type of mucker, an athlete who took money and exhibited a win-at-all-cost attitude. The gentleman athlete was expected to understand the written and unwritten rules of the game.

Hobey seemed surprised and uncomfortable with the publicity and attention that accompanied his remarkable skill on the ice. The Princeton team traveled via train to Montreal to play the McGill University squad during his junior year. The train pulled into the station in early morning, and to the surprise of the Tiger players, a crowd had already gathered in the station to greet the boy they had read so much about. As Hobey stepped off the train, cheers of "Hobey, Hobey" filled the air. He was besieged by Canadian fans clamoring for an autograph with many begging for one of his hockey sticks. A teammate later recalled how their timid captain seemed embarrassed at the greeting, but how proud they were to see that his fame had extended to the birthplace of ice hockey.

Those who witnessed Hobey play never failed to comment on his clean style of play and love of sportsmanship. As a wonder boy on the ice, the type of player who could alter the contest by himself, he was often the victim of vicious attacks. The newspapers reported that the word would go out to the opposing team before taking the ice, "Get Baker." If he couldn't be slowed down legally, then he was hooked to the ice or savagely slashed whenever he got near the puck. The helmet-less Hobey was tripped, cut, and beaten black and blue. Amazingly, this abuse only seemed to make him play harder, and when he retaliated, it was by scoring a goal. Baker was only penalized once in his entire college career.

One report described Baker being pushed over the boards and into the stands as he shot the puck behind the opponent's goal. The fans roared as he sprinted alongside of the rink on top of the boards, jumped back on the ice, grabbed the puck and scored a goal. Hobey's skating ability was so great and his turning ability so precise that sometimes even a clean opponent would inadvertently take a penalty against the speedy rover. A Harvard player who faced Baker on the ice remembered years later how the only penalty he took in his college hockey career was for tripping Hobey. He never forgot Baker, seeking him out after the contest and apologizing for drawing the penalty. Baker explained that he knew his opponent's record had been spotless and that his own balance was so delicate on a turn that the slightest touch would sometimes spill him. Another Harvard hockey player, Stuart Kaiser, wrote many years after his amateur career had ended that he could still hear the roar that would emerge from the Harvard side of the old Boston Arena when Hobey would take the puck from behind his own goal and skate it the length of the rink. He paid Baker the ultimate compliment when he recalled, "This was no enemy we were watching; we were looking at an unparalleled feat of magic artistry." No wonder that many of Baker's contemporaries saw him as the popular dime-novel hero Frank Merriwell come to life. When Merriwell stepped onto the gridiron or ice rink he, like Hobey, represented the best in sportsmanship, skill and strength of character.

The most famous Princeton game that Hobey took part in was one in which Harvard defeated the Tigers 2-1 in overtime. *The New York Times* described the game as one of the most desperately contested college hockey games in years, and it ended as the longest American college hockey game played up to that time.

The game took place at Boston Arena on Saturday, January 24, 1914. The scalpers experienced a windfall as everyone in Boston seemed to want a ticket. Gambling was at a fevered pitch, and the Tigers with Hobey were given 10-7 odds to win. Princeton suffered a bad break when two of its All-Star, starting wings were unable to play. Grant Peacock had a bad knee injury and E.B. Kilner was ineligible because of one too many chapel cuts. Princeton students were required to attend chapel during this period, and unlike the present-day college sports scene, an athlete, even an invaluable one, was expected to adhere to the rules.

The arena held six thousand people and every one of them, the majority of whom were Harvard fans, gave Hobey Baker a standing ovation when he took a few practice laps around the rink. Once the game began, it became apparent that the Tiger substitutes would be unable to keep up with the speedster Baker and his friend and sidekick, Wen Kuhn. Hobey's style of zigzagging and weaving in and around his opponent's defense would often inadvertently pull his own men "off sides." The no-forward passing rules of the day required the players not carrying the puck to stay behind their puck carrier or be called for an off sides play. Each time Baker took the puck up ice, the crowd would rise to its feet screaming, "Here he comes," as he attempted to score but was thwarted over and over again by the red-hot Harvard goaltender, "Guvvie" Carnochan, who played the game of his life that night in Boston Arena. The Harvard defense could not stop Hobey's rushes, and the newspaper later reported that the Tiger star was battering at the goal all evening.

The Tigers drew first-blood when Kuhn scored with a long shot from the left side. The Crimson seven answered almost immediately with a goal from M.B. Phillips. Hobey came close to winning the game as he broke up the ice but was hooked down before he launched his shot. The Harvard defenseman was penalized for the foul, but most observers of the game believed that the rule infraction probably saved the game for Harvard. Regulation play, two twenty-minute periods, would end in a 1-1 tie thanks to the Harvard goalie who stopped thirty-five Tiger shots, most of them from Baker and Kuhn. The Intercollegiate rules of the day called for two extra periods of five minutes with the teams changing goals for each period.

The iron-men battled through the two scoreless five minute periods when the team captains decided to play a "sudden-death" period. No one wanted to leave the ice since the rules of the era would not permit a player to return to the game after being replaced by a substitute. Amazingly, only five Harvard starters and one Tiger player required substitutes. All the others went the distance and Hobey was not even breathing heavily when he took the ice for the "sudden-death" period.

As fate would have it, it was one of the substitutes who would make history and end the marathon twenty-three minutes into the sudden-death period. Leverett Saltonstall, would never make a Harvard all-star team or be anything but a journeyman second-stringer, but that winter night in Boston he made Harvard history. The lumbering skater would one day tell his grandchildren about the night he took the ice against Hobey Baker and the champion Tiger team. Lev Saltonstall knew immediately that he was out of his league when he realized that even with fresh legs he was a step or two slower than the remaining starters who had been on the ice for over sixty punishing minutes. Like any player in that situation, he knew he did not want to be the goat that lost the game for the Crimson seven. As the twenty-three minute mark of the period approached, the speedy Harvard right wing Smart, corralled a rebound from his goalie and skated it down ice. His shot toward the Princeton goal was blocked by a Tiger defenseman, and the puck flew high into the air and fell at Saltonstall's feet. The nervous player lacked the confidence to skate the puck closer to the goal and opted to loft a low-percentage, twenty-five foot shot that miraculously scored. Leverett Saltonstall, who would later become governor of Massachusetts and serve as a United States Senator, loved to show his friends and family the treasured stick that he used in the Princeton-Harvard game.

Hobey and the Princeton Tigers proved just how talented a team they were in an amazing incident that took place in the winter of 1914. The team had just defeated the Harvard team 4-1, assuring them the 1913-1914 championship title. Baker tallied three assists and provided the show that the sold-out crowd at the St. Nicholas Rink had hoped to see. The majority of the spectators had attended for the purpose of seeing Baker go at top speed and he happily obliged them. Three of the goals were a result of Hobey skating the length of the rink and passing the puck from behind Harvard's goal to one of his slower teammates. The exhausted Harvard squad sent out five substitutes during the tilt while the Tigers went the distance with their original seven. The following morning, after most of the Princeton team had departed for home by train, the Tigers received a formal challenge from the mighty St. Nick's, the colorful semi-pro New York City team. Although short a man, Hobey accepted the challenge and the six weary Tigers miraculously defeated the well-rested St. Nick's seven in a 2-1 victory.

The Princeton team had been off the ice for less than an hour when they were again challenged. This time it was the powerful U.S. Army Seventh Regiment club that wanted a piece of the golden boy and his Princeton teammates. Still a man down and thoroughly exhausted, Hobey and his squad threw caution to the wind and laced up their skates. The Army team, with a man advantage during the entire forty minutes, suffered a humiliating 4-0 defeat at the hands of Hobey and company. The Princeton College boys and their shining star had defeated three formidable teams in less than twenty-four hours. That's a monumental accomplishment in any era, but when compared to today's professional hockey game, it takes on Herculean proportions. With four rotating lines and plenty of rest, courtesy of an abundance of commercial television breaks, twenty minutes of ice time for a professional player in a sixty-minute game is considered respectable. The legendary Princeton team played 120 minutes of no-substitute hockey in less than twenty-four hours, eighty of those minutes shorthanded, and remarkably defeated all challengers.

How good a hockey player was Hobey Baker? His stats speak for themselves. In his three seasons on the Princeton varsity team, he scored over 120 goals and over 100 assists. He averaged about three goals and three assists a game, a feat never equaled in college or professional hockey. A *New York Times* story once carried the headline, "Baker Shoots Eight Goals in Hockey Match." Hobey was an All-American three times in hockey and led the Tigers to two National Championships on the ice. Princeton's longest ice hockey winning streak, eleven games, took place during his sophomore and junior varsity seasons. He is the only amateur in both the Canadian and American Hockey Halls of Fame. Each year since 1981, the best college hockey player in America is awarded the Hobey Baker Memorial Award, the Heisman Trophy of hockey. While candidates are expected to demonstrate outstanding skills in all phases of the game, the primary requirement, a tribute to the coveted award's namesake, is that they must exhibit strength of character both on and off the ice.

Baker seated second from the right with the 1911-1912 Princeton Championship Hockey Team.

*"Oh, you and Princeton! You'd think that was the
world the way you talk!"*

F. Scott Fitzgerald, *This Side of Paradise*

Chapter Six

Hobey Baker graduated from Princeton University on
June 17, 1914 along with 231 classmates. They joined
the ranks of the four percent of Americans who held college degrees. Their class orator reminded them that along
with privilege came responsibility. He noted that "…great
problems are arising demanding immediate attention, and
it is the college-trained man who must contribute the prop-
er solution." The new alumni could feel confident in the
knowledge that the old guard was still securely entrenched
as evidenced by the presidential election of 1912 where the
three candidates, Taft, Roosevelt, and Wilson, were prod-
ucts respectively of Yale, Harvard and Princeton.

The class had entered the university as freshmen just
ten years into the new century. A reminder of their connection to the previous century came at the commencement
ceremony when the university conferred a degree on a gray-
haired, venerable Southerner who had left Princeton in his
junior year in 1861 to join the Confederate Army. His degree was given as of the Class of 1862.

The Class of 1914 had begun its scholastic journey
on the eve of the country's Age of Innocence and completed

it just as America and the rest of the world were about to grow up. A little more than a month after their graduation, a world war began in Europe when Archduke Franz Ferdinand, the heir to the Austrian throne, was assassinated along with his wife in Sarajevo. For the time being America remained neutral, and the sons of Nassau entered the world as the newest members of the old guard.

Hobart Amory Hare Baker had become the most famous amateur athlete in the country during his Princeton career. Although he did not choose to run for class office, he was an ex officio of the prestigious Senior Class Council because he had captained the football team. He was voted by his classmates, "The man who has done the most for Princeton." The adoring Princetonians bestowed other honors on him such as Best All-Around Athlete, Best Football Player, Best Hockey Player, and "the man who has done the most for the class in athletics." Hobey was every student's idol, the Prince of Princeton. He had proven that he was more than an athlete, earning a Bachelor of Letters degree, majoring in history, economics and politics. He graduated with a respectable *B* average. The summer after graduation was spent traveling through Europe as a celebrity correspondent for *The New York Times*. He reported on the Henley Regatta between Harvard and the best English varsity crew in London on July 19,1914, and declared that the American stroke was far superior to the English or European stroke. Hobey noted that he was so impressed with the Crimson crew's performance that he was almost willing to "forgive old John Harvard and let bygones be bygones." Although his fame presented the twenty-two-year old athlete with opportunities like *The New York Times'* summer position, he would eventually come to detest what he later referred to as his, "cheap newspaper name."

Hobey had been an athletic god from the day he entered St. Paul's at age 12 until his graduation from Princeton at age 22. With his academic career behind him, Hobey had to think about earning a living and getting on with his life. Unlike many of his former classmates, he could not rely on a wealthy family for support. He could, however, make use of the Princeton network and secure a Wall Street position at Johnson and Higgins, a large Manhattan insurance firm. He eventually had a new door opened by another son of Nassau and moved on to J.P. Morgan Bank at One Wall Street to begin a two-year trainee program. His twenty-dollar a week salary was about twenty percent less than a Ford factory worker could make on the Model T assembly line.

Reports indicate that Hobey was a conscientious but restless junior executive. The Princeton Tiger was caged in a corporate mailroom, and friends sensed that he longed to break free. He dreamed of returning to the gridiron when he read the newspaper reports of the dedication of the colossal 61,000 seat Yale Bowl. Hobey regretted that he would never have the opportunity to play in this magnificent shrine to the secular religion that college football had become. It is easy to imagine that F. Scott Fitzgerald, a lifelong admirer of Baker, had Hobey in mind when in *The Great Gatsby*, he described the fictitious, former Ivy-League football star, Tom Buchanan, as "a national figure in a way, one of those men who reach such an acute limited excellence at twenty-one that everything afterwards savours of anti-climax."

Hobey was temporarily rescued from his routine existence by the colorful Percy Rivington Pyne, II, the poster boy for the idle rich. Percy invited Hobey to reside at his home located at 263 Madison Avenue in New York City and Baker accepted. The two began a friendship that would last until Hobey's untimely death in 1918. Although Pyne was ten years Baker's senior, they were both card-carrying members of the old boys club. Like Baker, Percy was a graduate of St. Paul's and Princeton, and they both belonged to Ivy, the first and most prestigious Princeton eating club. Percy religiously maintained his old school ties and had met Hobey during one of his frequent visits to St. Paul's while the young athlete was still a student.

Percy's father, the exceptionally wealthy Moses Taylor Pyne (Princeton 1877), was a trustee and the principal benefactor of the university. Moses was instrumental in the transition of Princeton from college to university, and during his thirty-six years on the Board of Trustees he did not miss a meeting. Should anyone doubt the Pyne Princeton pedigree, he need only look at Percy's address during his undergraduate years, 2 Upper Pyne Building, or visit The Pyne Library or Pyne Tower on campus. The Pyne estate, Drumthwacket, was the center of social life for Princeton during the Pyne era. Today, the stately mansion is the New Jersey Governor's residence. So well-loved was Percy's father, that on the day of his funeral Princeton classes were canceled, and commerce stopped on Nassau Street in his memory.

Percy possessed the wealth that had eluded the Baker family, and Hobey possessed the athletic prowess that was the envy of Percy and all who came in contact with him. A biography of Percy in the *Twenty-Year Record of the Class of 1903* noted that he was "entitled to wear Varisty 'P',"as the captain of the varsity golf team. He basked in the glow of Hobey's celebrity, and the young banker took advantage of the good life that Pyne's money and prestige could provide. The-larger-than-life New York socialite belonged to thirty-seven clubs and served on the board of scores of corporations. Following in the footsteps of his father, he was elected a Life Member of the Board of Trustees of Princeton University.

Percy threw legendary parties, and the impressionable Baker found himself in the midst of New York's elite society. Several years later when Hobey was stationed in Europe, he would confirm the effect that the Pyne lifestyle had on him when complaining in a letter about his Spartan existence in Paris. "You see, it is all your fault, you started me in all these expensive habits, " he good-naturedly admonished Percy. Hobey would later fly alongside the legendary ace Eddie Rickenbacker during the war, and the two pilots would enjoy reminiscing about competing in Percy Pyne's Metropolitan 300, a race that Eddie had won in his Maxwell Special automobile. The Metropolitan 300 provided an opportunity for the victor to claim over $25,000 in prize money and was one of the most prestigious races of the era, rivaling the Vanderbilt Cup. Run at Sheepshead Bay in Long Island, New York, the race attracted the best drivers in the world. The field included competitors such as Dario Resta, Johnny Aitken and Carl Limberg in the year Rickenbacker won. During the race, Limberg and his mechanic skidded into a wall, and both were killed instantly. Rickenbacker, a fierce competitor, was the first driver to see the tragic accident, and he memorized the position of the fiery wreck. On the next lap, as the other drivers slowed down to investigate, Rickenbacker blew through the smoke-engulfed conflagration and gained enough time to win the contest. The Metropolitan 300 was the type of activity that Percy Pyne enjoyed sponsoring and Hobey Baker lived to participate in.

Social selection manifested itself at the end of the nineteenth century in the form of elite eating clubs. The first club, Ivy, was created in 1878 and was the most prestigious of the Princeton clubs. During the era when Baker attended Old Nassau, the university only provided food services for freshmen and sophomores. Upperclassmen had to fend for themselves and those who were connected joined the various eating clubs. Hobey, along with other St. Paul's boys, joined Ivy in his junior year.

What is this life if, full of care,
We have no time to stand and stare

William Henry Davies, *Leisure*

Chapter Seven

With no established professional hockey teams in the United States during the latter part of the nineteenth century, amateur leagues and teams began to spring up in the major eastern cities. Many followed the lead of the Canadian amateur leagues where wealthy gentlemen sportsmen battled each other on the ice for the enjoyment of their well-heeled friends and business associates. The first indoor rink in New York City was the old Ice Palace, located at 107th Street and Lexington Avenue. It opened in the early 1890's, and in a short while local hockey clubs began friendly rivalries. The games shifted to the Clermont Avenue Rink in Brooklyn and eventually to the St. Nicholas Skating Rink, located a block from Central Park at 66th Street and Columbus Avenue. The St. Nicholas Skating Club was soon founded, and prominent New Yorkers such as Cornelius Vanderbilt, John Jacob Astor and J. Piermont Morgan, could be seen enjoying an evening skate in the beautiful new facility. Indoor ice-skating was at that time an activity for the wealthy and socially prominent.

A year after the rink was constructed, the St. Nicholas Hockey Club was organized. The club was the creation of hockey pioneer and enthusiast, Kenneth Gordon, and it quickly developed a following in the sports hungry metropolis. The Amateur Hockey League was originally composed of the New York Athletic Club, the Brooklyn Skating Club, the Hockey Club of New York and the St. Nick's. The Vanderbilt and Astor clan, in an effort to preserve the venue for the monied class, set the admission at one dollar in an era when the average working man earned twenty dollars a week.

With the creation of the Intercollegiate Hockey League in 1900, the St. Nick's or the "Santa Claus Organization," as the press was fond of calling it, along with the other amateur hockey clubs, found worthy opponents among the elite eastern universities to battle on the ice. The college league also served as an incubator for future St. Nick's players. No stranger to the St. Nicholas Rink, Hobey Baker, along with his St. Paul's prep school squad, had played the St. Nick's in a memorable game there in 1908. Lacking a rink of its own, the Princeton University varsity hockey team played many of its games in the rink during Baker's college career.

The roster of the St. Nick's squad consisted almost entirely of Ivy League graduates with a handful of Canadian semi-pros. The St. Nick's provided an opportunity for the recent graduates to stay in shape while maintaining their old school ties. A competitive tradition quickly took hold between elite university teams and their alums on the St. Nick's. The games became a social event, and when Manhattan society turned out for a game, the ice rink more often resembled an opera house than a hockey venue. Lines of limousines and carriages surrounded the rink when an Ivy team came to town. The Big Three students and alums would travel by train to see their current team battle the St. Nick's. It was with great excitement that the press announced in 1914 that Hobey Baker would don the red and green uniform of the Santa Claus Organization for the 1914-1915 season. Rumors had circulated that the former Princeton star might move to Boston after graduation to play for the mighty Boston Amateur Athletic squad, but New York City fans rejoiced when Hobey reported to the St. Nicholas Rink for his first team practice. The Boston team had just been admitted to the league, and the St. Nick's along with the other teams knew that they needed to reinforce their squads to take on this new, formidable foe. Wendell Kuhn, one of Hobey's closest friends and a St. Paul's and Princeton teammate during Baker's career, along with another St. Paul's alum and former Harvard star, William Willetts, both joined the St. Nick's. The newspapers pronounced that with Baker, Kuhn and Willetts joining the Santa Claus Organization, the New York seven would have a genuine chance at winning the league championship. A few additional former Ivy-League stars, Carnochan, (Harvard), Trimble and Von Bermuth (Columbia) and Cox and Martin (Yale) fortified the squad. Professional hockey teams from the fledgling Canadian leagues traveled to Manhattan to scout the young star and pronounced to the local press that Baker was fast enough to claim a spot on any team in Canada. The St. Nick's that year played in the American Amateur Hockey League consisting of the Irish-American Athletic Club, the Crescent Athletic Club, the Boston Athletic Club and others. The winner of the league championship would face the Canadian amateur champions in an international exhibition game for that year's bragging rights.

The league promoters quickly realized the drawing potential of the former Tiger star as each game of the season was played before sell-out crowds. He was the country's first marquee player, and the St. Nick's management responded by posting a sign outside the rink, "Hobey Baker Plays Here Tonight." Uncomfortable with his fame and always concerned about his teammates, Hobey insisted that the sign come down. Legend states that on numerous occasions he would refuse to play until the promoters agreed to his request. A local paper estimated that at least half of the crowd at every game came to see Baker. Hobey had the ability to bring the audience to near hysteria whenever he began one of his patented sorties down the ice. Women and men would take to their feet screaming, "Here he comes," as the golden-haired jet took two quick strides and blasted past his opponents.

Aware of his fans' expectations, Hobey began his quest for the league championship. Baker learned a painful lesson during that historic season: he was no longer in a gentleman's league, and sportsmanship to many of his competitors meant winning at all cost. His fame preceded him and, sadly, the strategy throughout the league was to hurt Baker. While he did not wear a number on his jersey, he often felt as if he had a bull's-eye painted on his back. He was tripped, slashed, speared and cut throughout the grueling season. Always the sportsman, Hobey played through the rough stuff as best he could. One report noted, "Baker was so marvelous that he was early selected as the victim of tripping and of vicious swipes at his head with sticks, but he calmly evaded the unwholesome designs of his opponents, and was going as strong at the end as when the game started." He seemed to possess an inner strength that kept him skating when others would have quit, and as an amateur, he was not being paid to receive these nightly vicious beatings.

One game in particular stood out for its intense brutality toward Hobey when the St. Nick's played against the champion Victorias from Canada. The champs were playing for payback as Baker's team had previously beaten the highly favored University of Toronto squad in a hotly contested 7-6 tilt with Hobey embarrassing the Toronto seven, scoring five goals and assisting on the other two.

The St. Nick's -Victorias' game was so ugly that a New York newspaper wrote that the reason Canadian hockey players had not enlisted in Canada's brave contingent fighting in the Great War in Europe was that they had already shed enough blood on the ice to satisfy them. The report went on to say that so brutal was the beating Baker received on the ice by the Canadian players that a disgusted New

York fan in the stands shouted, "Why don't you get a club and finish the task quickly?" Unfortunately, a club was not needed after a Canadian player cut Hobey's leg with the edge of his skate. A later edition of the newspaper reported that Baker's cut was clean and was healing nicely. The paper called for the attacker to be banned from hockey for life. Hobey had exacted his revenge, scoring four of the six St. Nick's goals in their 6-1 victory. The newspaper headline summed up his performance, "Hobey Baker Defeats Victoria Seven."

An incident that season in Boston illustrated how much Hobey was loved and respected in the league. The St. Nick's were playing the Boston Athletic Association when Hobey was tripped by a local player and sent hard to the ice. Baker hit the back of his head and experienced a minor concussion accompanied by several minutes of unconsciousness. The Boston crowd was so respectful of Hobey and his clean style of play that they booed their offending hometown skater every time he touched the puck for the balance of the evening.

In a key game between the first-place St. Nick's and the second-place Irish-American Athletic Club, two hired guns on the Irish squad caused a pre-game stir by promising in a newspaper story to stop Baker. A few minutes into the game it became apparent to the tough guys that there was no legal way to slow down the fleet-footed Baker. As the game clock ticked away the final few seconds of the contest, the St. Nick's were in the lead. One of the two hit men in a desperate act pulled Hobey's skates out from under him and sent the star sliding into the iron post of the goal. This was years before breakaway posts held the goal in place, so slamming into the iron post was akin to hitting a cement wall. Baker lay motionless and many of the spectators feared that he had broken his neck. He slowly rose to his feet after a few terrifying minutes and skated to the locker room. Regretting his behavior toward the St. Nick's star, the player who had tripped Hobey would always

remember how after the game, he summoned up the courage to visit Baker's locker room. He timidly apologized for
his cheap shot, and to his great surprise, Hobey, always the
sportsman, flashed his famous smile and offered the dejected player his hand. He told him that he wasn't sure what
had occurred in the heat of the action and for all he knew
he might have tripped on the defenseman's stick. For the
rest of his life, the player would remember that memorable
encounter with the charismatic superstar.

Baker's personality had dominated the entire hockey season. The slightest rumor that an injury might prevent him from playing during the regular season prompted
hundreds of phone calls to the team's management. The
fans came to see Hobey. Throughout the punishing season Hobey remained the ultimate gentleman athlete and
was only penalized once during his entire St. Nick's career.
The predictions that his addition to the team would bring
a championship to the boys in the red and green sweat-
ers proved accurate. The championship game was played
between the St. Nick's and the Boston Athletic Association.
Hobey was unstoppable, and before the contest ended, the
speedy rover would have a hand in four of the St. Nick's five
goals. The headlines read, "Hobey Baker Wins the Hockey
Championship," and proclaimed that Baker was the greatest amateur hockey star of the age. The sportswriters unanimously agreed that when it came to pure talent and determination, Hobey Baker was to hockey what Ty Cobb was to
baseball. In story after story they would praise his unassum-
ing, happy-go-lucky attitude and his almost obsessive desire
to avoid publicity. As a skater, stick-handler, goal scorer and
all-around athlete, he was in a league of his own.

With the league championship secured, the St.
Nick's accepted challenges from two different Canadian
teams. The first game was with the highly rated Argonauts
of Toronto, a squad made up of former Canadian college
stars. The Argonauts were certain they were prepared for
Baker and used a well-oiled, tight-checking defensive sys-

tem to stop the winged skater. It failed and Baker sent them packing.

The final meeting against a Canadian club that year was a post-season exhibition contest played between the St. Nick's and the St. Miguel's, the fearless amateur champions of Ontario. Baker and company won easily with a score of 5-1, and hockey writers and players north of the border began to take more notice of the wonder boy of amateur hockey. Hobey had provided the record crowd with a memorable show, and as one sportswriter commented, "Baker did all that was expected of him and skimmed over the ice phantom-like, out-skating all of his opponents."

One spectator at the game was Harry Hyland, the captain of the Wanderers, a professional Canadian hockey team. Hyland and his mates were in New York City to play a series against their rivals, the Canadiens at the St. Nicholas Rink. In a newspaper story the day after the St. Nick's victory, Hyland told reporters that Hobey stood so far above other American players that to make comparisons would be ridiculous. He commented that Baker could sign and play with the Wanderers or any other professional team. Hyland added, " The thing that struck me most was his speed. That is the great asset in the money play."

The following season looked like a promising one for the fledgling sport with *The New York Times* proclaiming, "Amateur Hockey To Have a Big Year." The league received a boost when the Harvard Club of Boston joined the Amateur Hockey League. The Harvard Club team drew from many former Harvard University stars and along with the Boston Athletic Association promised to increase the intra-city rivalry in the league. The pundits were in agreement that amateur hockey players in the United States were now at the same level as their brothers north of the border.

Spurred on by this sentiment, Cornelius Fellowes, the ambitious proprietor of the St. Nicholas Rink, was finally successful, after several false starts the previous season, in arranging a series between Hobey Baker's St. Nick's, the reigning Amateur Hockey League champions; and the Montreal Stars, the Eastern Canadian champs. At stake would be the Art Ross Trophy, which at the time was emblematic of the championship of Eastern Canada. *The Art Ross Trophy was donated by its namesake to the NHL in 1947 to be awarded to the NHL's scoring leader each season.* Never before had an amateur team from the United States had an opportunity to claim such a major international prize. Ever the showman, Fellowes arranged the series as a best of three: game one to begin in Montreal; game two to be played in New York City where it would also mark the beginning of the 1915 hockey season. Hockey at that time was played with six men per team in Canada and seven men per team in the United States. The Canadian system had eliminated the rover position, and their teams consisted of a goalie, two wings, two defensemen and a centerman. This complement would eventually become the standard for both amateur and professional hockey throughout the world.

The rules for the series were set. Game one, played on December 11th, in Montreal, would be played with seven men; game two, scheduled for December 18th, in New York City, would be played with six skaters; and if necessary, game three on December 20th, also played in New York, would feature seven men in the first twenty-minute period and six men in the final half. The first game in Montreal was played before the largest crowd that had ever witnessed an amateur game in Montreal Arena. The Stars took the challenge from the St. Nick's too lightly and before they knew it, found themselves on a train to New York City, contemplating how this upstart team of former college boys had embarrassed them in front of their fans. The final score was 6-2 in favor of the St. Nick's. *The New York Times* headline read, "Play of St. Nick's Baffles Canadians," and as expected, the former Princeton star delivered, scoring two of the goals and assisting on three others.

The excitement spread throughout New York City and the rest of the nation for one more victory would claim the cup from the country that had invented hockey. The game was played before a sell-out crowd, and even standing room tickets were sold at a premium. Hockey enthusiasts along with the sportswriters agreed that the tilt was one of the most exciting hockey games ever played between the two countries. Hobey was at his best, and if he demonstrated a weakness, it was that he was so fast the other forwards could not keep up with him. A sportswriter reported that Baker was often compelled to make his own plays unassisted due to his lightning speed. The Stars brought their "A" game to New York and both teams seemed equally matched. The Canadians targeted Baker and the press reported that "the visitors seldom lost an opportunity to cover the fastest and best player in American amateur ranks." Three penalties were taken by the Stars in their unsuccessful efforts to stop Hobey's whirlwind rushes.

The score was 2-2 at the end of regulation play and since a third extra period produced no scoring, the game ended in a tie. The game was surrounded in controversy and many of the spectators believed that the game and therefore the Ross Cup had been stolen from the St. Nick's when Hobey's winning goal was recalled by Referee Samuels of Montreal, who decided, according to *The New York Times*, "…that the rubber stopped a trifle short of the goal." There was no video play review in 1915. Hobey was proclaimed the star of the game and the headline read, "Baker Saves Team In Hockey Game."

With the series knotted at 1-1, the final game was played at the St. Nicholas Rink for the cup. The Stars, realizing that they had dodged a bullet in the previous contest, stepped up their game and again targeted Canada's public enemy number one, Hobart Hare Amory Baker. Hockey is a rough game, and it is not unusual for even the most sportsman-like player to lose his temper in the heat of battle. Unfortunately, a stick can be almost lethal in the right hands, and that night Hobey was tripped, slashed, cut, speared and given the "short end of the stick" until he could barely stand. He received a particularly nasty blow across the nose with a stick that left him stunned and required play to be suspended until he could recover. Fancy stick work in the hands of an expert can go undetected by the officials, yet the short end of the stick, the section above the hands, can leave its victim with a painful reminder of the contest for weeks.

Unfortunately, as in the second game of the season, Hobey's speed was as detrimental to the St. Nick's as it was to the Montreal Stars. A sportswriter who covered the game wrote that "Baker's speed ruined many plays as the forwards were unable to keep up with the ex-Princeton star." He often found himself alone in his opponent's territory with his teammates struggling to keep up with him. The Stars won the game by a score of 2-1. Under the rules of competition for the Cup, a tie counts as a victory for the defending team, so the reigning champions boarded a train for Montreal, cup in hand as the sports headlines proclaimed, "Art Ross Trophy Goes To Canada."

The same newspapers carried headlines of a more ominous nature at the same time the St. Nick's – Montreal Stars series took place. The Cunard liner *Lusitania* was torpedoed by a German U-boat in the Irish Sea. The luxury liner sank in less than twenty minutes sending 1,198 men, women and children to the sea's bottom. Among the dead were 128 Americans, and the appalling loss of life caused angry citizens of all classes to call for their neutral government to enter the Great War raging in Europe. The horrific carnage had reached a stalemate in the godless trenches of the Western Front, yet both sides continued to send wave after wave of soldiers forward in a fruitless effort to gain an advantage. The loss of life was unfathomable and as the war raged on, the life of a gentleman athlete skating for New York society and hobnobbing with the likes of Percy Pyne seemed insignificant to the twenty-three-year old athlete.

The roster of the St. Nick's amateur team consisted almost entirely of Ivy League graduates with a handful of Canadian semi-pros. Their league provided spectator hockey for New York City fans in the era before professional hockey was established in the United States. The St. Nick's would often challenge their former Ivy League teams to games that were the toast of the town. Hobey is seated second from the left.

Man's Character is his Fate

Heraclitus

Chapter Eight

Hobey played hockey with the St. Nick's after the 1915 season, but his heart was no longer in the game. The sport that he had loved all his life had grown less sportsmanlike each season, and the "get Baker" tactics were taking a toll on his battered body. He was offered a great deal of money to play professional hockey, but the former Princeton Tiger wanted no part of the professional game. Professional hockey was in its infancy, and sportsmen felt that the professional game would ruin their beloved ice hockey as they believed it was already destroying baseball, America's national pastime. Ever the gentleman athlete, Baker was part of a generation who believed that accepting money for sports was a sacrilege. In Hobey's world, the true athlete played sport for the love of the game. He laced up the skates for the last time in February 1917, scoring his final goal in an uninspired contest between the St. Nick's and a Canadian team, the Aura Lee Club. Baker's team lost 2-1.

The Great War in Europe that began as a series of blunders fueled by shortsighted diplomats seeking to further their national interests in what they believed would be an unsustainable, short-lived conflict had entered its second year in 1915 with no end in sight. The Allies – Britain, France, Russia and Italy – would sustain almost twenty-five million casualties before the armistice. The Central Powers – chiefly Germany, Austria-Hungary, and Turkey – would sustain fifteen million casualties before it was over.

When the war broke out in Europe, America with its millions of new immigrants took a non-judgmental position. The new Americans came from both the Central Powers and the Allies, and their president, Woodrow Wilson, promised to keep the United States out of war. Early into the conflict, America's neutrality began to wane when the British, the master of the seas, cut Germany's Atlantic cable and took control of much of the information America received concerning the war. The lingering depression that America had been experiencing was reversed by the war. Loans to the Allies generated huge profits for the likes of J.P. Morgan's National City Bank, and prosperity swept the country. A deadly British blockade ground the Germans' invasion of France to a halt. The Germans' response to the effective blockade was an escalation in their U-boat warfare, which appeared inhuman and pushed the Americans toward the Allies' cause. Although both the Allies and Central Powers were guilty of nationalistic aggression at its worst, the Germans had lost the propaganda war and in doing so had lost the hearts of the American people. The 1910 census documented that one of every three Americans was either foreign born or the child of a foreign born parent. Over ten million Americans had emigrated from the Central Powers, Germany and Austria-Hungary. Life suddenly became uncomfortable for hyphenated Americans with foreign accents. Overnight sauerkraut became "liberty cabbage" and dachshunds were renamed "victory pups."

Many idealistic young Americans of Hobey's generation, believing that France was a victim, had joined the conflict years before the United States entered the war. They came in large numbers from the Ivy League universities, students of privileged families seeking to fulfill their *noblesse oblige.* One such individual was Alan Seeger, a 1910 graduate of Harvard, who in August 1914 joined the French Foreign Legion in order to fight for the Allies against the Central Powers. Enlistment in the Foreign Legion provided a legal mechanism for eager American volunteers to fight for the French. Barely forty-eight hours after the war had begun in Europe, Myron Herrick, the American Ambassador to France, was besieged by young Americans eager to fight but concerned about the legality of joining another country's army. Herrick and his staff perused the books regarding such matters and advised the young men that enlistment in the French Army would cost them their citizenship. He then lifted their spirits by noting that enlistment in the Foreign Legion would carry little risk of forfeiting their American citizenship. The reason was a technicality. The enlistment contract with the Foreign Legion did not require the volunteer to swear an oath of allegiance to France. This "loophole" permitted forty-three Americans, including Seeger, to take part in an historic ceremony on August 21, 1914, in the courtyard of the Hotel des Invalides in Paris, where they were sworn in as privates in the Legion.

Seeger chose the hard life of an infantryman and lost his life in the historic Battle of the Somme, where over 80,000 men were killed or wounded on the first day of the offensive. A writer and poet, he documented his experiences in letters sent home to family and newspapers. He ended the last letter sent home on June 28, 1916, with the words, "I am glad to be going in the first wave. If you are in this thing at all, it is best to be in to the limit. And this is the supreme experience." In the final stanza of his most famous poem, *"I Have A Rendezvous With Death...."*, he wrote prophetically,

> *God knows 'twere better to be deep*
> *Pillowed in silk and scented down,*
> *Where Love throbs out in blissful sleep,*
> *Pulse nigh to pulse, and breath to breath,*

Where hushed awakenings are dear...
But I've a rendezvous with Death
At midnight in some flaming town,
When Spring trips north again this year,
And I to my pledged word am true,
I shall not fail that rendezvous.

Inspired by men like Alan Seeger to make a differ-
ence in the war, Hobey grew more restless by the day and
had neither the wealth nor the inclination to pursue the
dilettante lifestyle that his mentor Percy Pyne had spent
years perfecting. One of Percy's uninspiring claims to fame,
while men like Alan Seeger sacrificed their lives for their
beliefs, was to establish a policy at one of his exclusive clubs
to make six-course meals available twenty-four hours a day.

Wall Street would never appease Hobey's romantic
spirit, so along with many of his fellow countrymen, he
looked to the skies over Europe to begin his great adventure.
As America inched closer to joining the terrible conflagration in Europe, the country had only twenty-four combat-
ready pilots available for air service. What the United States
did not lack was a supply of young men eager to volunteer
to become modern-day knights of the air. Only a dozen or
so years earlier, flying machines were considered novelties,
as the world watched Orville Wright and his brother Wilbur
take flight in their "machine" on a December afternoon
in 1903 near Kittyhawk, N.C. Early in the war, the military
strategists refused to accept the airplane as a serious part of
their offense or defense. As the war progressed, aircraft was
used for observation purposes, and there were many documented instances of a lone airman saving thousands of lives
by sighting an advancing army where some bureaucrat's
map claimed it was not supposed to be. Machine guns were
mounted at first on top of the planes, and later techno-
logical advances permitted synchronized machine guns to
shoot through whirling propeller blades as a daring knight

of the air swooped down on his prey. By 1916, the military brass had a change of heart and a good air-pilot was considered of equal value to a battalion of troops. The sky was now the precious "high ground" that generals had sought from the time man first went to war.

In 1917, over 38,000 Americans would volunteer to sit on top of a highly explosive fuel tank in a wicker seat attached to a magic machine that had a hardwood skeleton, skin made of oil-coated, hand-sewn linen and the power of 220 horses. The aero service would soon become the new cavalry. The horse soldier of the Old West and of Teddy Roosevelt's famous Rough Riders had no place in this new kind of war. A March 1918 description by William Pressey of a French cavalry encounter with a machine gun documents the death knell of the old romantic cavalry in war. Pressey described how the French horsemen, believing they were pursuing a German cavalry unit on the other side of a hill, met the twentieth century head-on. "Coming towards us were (sic) a troop of French cavalry. I should say a hundred and fifty or two hundred strong. Gosh they looked splendid," Pressey wrote. He went on to describe the proud soldiers with their lances gleaming in the sunlight, as they went over the top of a hill and ran into a horrific new technology, a German machine gunner. A hellish sound echoed through the quiet woods, the sound of human slaughter, and in a minute it was over. A few rider-less horses meandered back across the hill. It was clear the new cavalry would be the air squadron, and it would do battle in the air away from the mud, barbed wire and endless miles of trenches.

Just as idealistic Americans such as Alan Seeger had entered the war ahead of their country, a few pioneer aviators had found the means to fly with the French Aviation Service. Some were civilians, some were battle-weary infantrymen who had fought with the Foreign Legion, some were fearless ambulance drivers who had volunteered for service in the American Ambulance unit. The catalyst for this group was Norman Prince, a wealthy pioneer aviator, who felt great love and passion for the French people and wished to assist them in their time of need. He dreamed of organizing an aero squadron composed exclusively of Americans. The result was the famous Escadrille Americaine, consisting originally of Prince and six other Americans: William Thaw, Victor Chapman, Kiffin Rockwell, James McConnell, Bert Hall and Elliot Cowdin. The fledgling group of warriors received financial support from millionaire William K. Vanderbilt, who opposed America's neutral stance. The squadron was given the official designation of N. 124 by the French government and was formed on April 20, 1916. The Escadrille Americaine was commanded by French officer Captain Georges Thenault, and it quickly became one of the most famous air squadrons in the sky. The group flew its first mission in May 1916, and former infantryman, Kiffin Rockwell, scored its first documented kill, taking down a German reconnaissance aircraft. The Escadrille Americaine eventually experienced a name change as the result of a German government protest to the still neutral United States Government. In December 1916, the French changed the name of the Escadrille Americaine to the Escadrille Lafayette, in honor of General Lafayette, the French officer who assisted the United States during the American Revolution. The story of an American squadron fighting for France in a war in which its country was still neutral captivated every armchair warrior from New York to California. The Escadrille's dangerous exploits along with its mascots, two lion cubs named Whiskey and Soda, provided miles of newspaper copy. While thousands of soldiers were living, fighting and dying in miles of rat-infested, muddy trenches, some no more than cesspools of stagnant water, the modern day knights flew in the bright sunlight miles above the squalor and death. An infantryman was an anonymous soldier, one of millions, but a pilot was an individual, with a plane bearing his squadron's insignia and often his name. They were the gentlemen warriors, killers with Ivy- League manners (four of the original seven members of the squadron were graduates of Harvard and Yale), and the courage of winged lions.

With little progress taking place in the trenches below, a kill in the sky became newsworthy, and German, French, Italian and English daredevils became media stars. They were combatants with household names, and the newspapers quickly realized that the flyboys' exploits sold papers. The Central Powers' pilots rode their *Albatross* and *Fokker D* planes into battle, while the Allies countered with their *S.P.A.D.*, *Nieuport* and *Sopwith Camel* stallions of the sky. A new language was created to describe the life of a pilot. A shoot-out in the sky was a *dogfight,* and a pilot's cockpit was his *office.* An observation balloon was a *sausage* and the plane's control lever a *joy stick.* Every schoolboy dreamed of becoming an *ace,* a designation for a pilot with at least five confirmed kills. One of the original members of the Lafayette Escadrille, Victor Emmanuel Chapman, had attended St. Paul's with Baker. Hobey grew more restless with Wall Street as he, along with eager newspaper readers throughout the world, followed the thrilling exploits of Chapman and the Escadrille.

"Be Prepared," became the watchword of America in the years before the country entered the war. Hobey began his love affair with the airplane and began taking lessons at Governor's Island every day in a Curtiss military biplane. His fame was such that a newspaper story ran the headline, "U.S. Preparedness Wave Gets Hobey Baker For Aviator Corps." "Yes, I have taken up flying," he told the reporter. "I decided recently in conjunction with a number of other college men to undergo military preparation in accordance with the idea of preparedness." He added, "Aviation appealed to me more than any other branch of the service." Baker had found a substitute for the excitement of the gridiron and the ice rink and an antidote for life in the office. He told the reporter that he was flying everyday that he could get away from business in time to make it to Governor's Island by 4 PM. He also noted that although there was a "sporting side" to flying, it was the serious side and preparedness for the United States that interested him and his friends. The reporter went on to mention that over seventy-five percent of the men who had volunteered for training were actively interested in some type of sport and that the World War had proved the value of the athlete. The sentiment was clear; the lessons required to make men out of office workers were acquired on the playing field.

The same article ran a poem that captured the country's mood:

> *God grant us that the roar of hostile guns,*
> *Shall not disturb this land's tranquility;*
> *God grant that we shall never have to face*
> *A hostile fleet upon the rolling sea.*
> *God grant we never view in skies above*
> *A battle of the birdmen of the air-*
> *But in a world gone mad with deeds of blood,*
> *LET US PREPARE!*

By November 1916, six months before America would enter the war on the side of the Allies, Hobey was still playing the occasional game with the St. Nick's. He had spurned numerous offers to turn professional and continued to devote most of his free time to flying. On November 18th, Hobey led a squadron of twelve airplanes in military formation from the United States aviation field in Mineola, New York to Princeton, New Jersey, where the annual Yale-Princeton game was about to be played. *The New York Times* documented the event in great detail. The festive collegians were preparing for the most popular game of the season when their former star and eleven other pilots appeared out of the autumn clouds and treated them to a pre-game air show. The students rose to their feet and cheered the blonde wonder boy as he and his fellow daredevil pilots executed heart-stopping maneuvers above Palmer Stadium. They dipped, spiraled and performed flawless loop the loops. The "Football Special," as the squadron was quickly named, consisted of airplanes from both Mineola and Governor's Island. The fanciful flight was a combination of work and pleasure as the cross-country exercise fulfilled a military requirement. Hobey's and another plane flew from Governor's Island while the others started from Mineola. An observer with strong field glasses was assigned to watch for the ten Mineola crafts, and once they were spotted, Hobey and the other pilot took to the air and fell into formation. The twelve machines made history as they constituted the largest number ever to fly in military formation. One of Baker's fellow pilots was the brother of William Thaw, a charter member of the Escadrille Americaine. Hobey, who had just received his preliminary certificate as a government aviator, was also the first to land his aircraft that memorable afternoon at Princeton. This established another record: the first American to reach a football game by air route, a fitting honor for the country's most beloved amateur athlete.

Hobey and his fellow airmen stole the show as they eventually climbed to their seats in the grandstand, still wearing their regulation leather coats and flying suits. Women crowded around the gentleman warriors and men envied these young eagles. The blonde-haired hero, who had for years treated his throngs of admirers to superhuman feats on the gridiron and ice, had now donned wings and defied gravity. His fans eagerly anticipated Hobey's triumphs in the sky.

The World Must be Safe for Democracy

Woodrow Wilson

Chapter Nine

Woodrow Wilson's first term as president of the United States ended as the Great War was raging in Europe. Reformation of the existing currency and banking laws through the Federal Reserve Act and a strengthening of antitrust legislation via the Federal Trade Commission Act and the Clayton Anti-Trust Act were among his numerous achievements. In 1916, the 28th president of the United States signed into law the Federal Farm Loan Act that provided farmers with affordable, low-interest credit. Added to these accomplishments were labor reform and the introduction of the income tax. Most historians believe Wilson was on his way to establishing himself as a great president.

Notwithstanding these first-term achievements, it was the progressive commander-in-chief's efforts to keep America neutral during the bloody conflagration overseas that established his popularity across the nation. The campaign slogan, "He kept us out of war," guaranteed him a victory in the 1916 presidential election and sent him to the White House for another four years. Most Americans believed that the carnage occurring thousands of miles away from their homeland had nothing to do with them.

This was despite the fact that America was riding the crest of an unprecedented wave of immigration, and millions of first-and second-generation immigrants hailed from both warring sides.

When the war began in the summer of 1914, Kaiser Wilhelm II of Germany was so confident that his country would achieve a speedy victory that he boasted to his staff, "Paris for lunch, dinner in St. Petersburg." The much vaunted Schlieffen Plan called for the fearsome German army to circumvent France's line of forts, swing through neutral Belgium, and turn south in a huge arc through France. The theory was that the French army would be destroyed defending Paris, and the war would be over by Christmas.

The image of the savage Hun was born as the tiny, antiquated Belgian army valiantly resisted the German troops, the mightiest army in the world. After crushing the Belgian armed forces with a barrage of one-ton shells thanks to Big Bertha, the largest cannon in existence, the Germans were surprised by a civilian population who launched a sniper campaign against the invaders. Retaliation was swift, and the Germans carried through on a promise to kill ten civilians for every soldier shot by a Belgian sniper. Hundreds of men, women and children were lined up and massacred. The British and American press began a massive propaganda campaign and the story of poor "little Belgium" fighting the "Huns" for their survival resonated throughout Europe and neutral America.

Early in the war, the flow of trade from the United States to the warring powers began to favor the Allies. A robust supply of gold and favorable shipping made it more reliable and profitable to do business with the Allies. By 1917, American banks had made over $2.5 billion in loans to the Allies, and American industrial giants had sold over $2 billion in goods to them. Slowly but surely, the fate of the fragile American economy became linked to an Ally victory.

The antiquated nineteenth century rules of engagement had been altered by the Germans with the introduction of the aerial bombing of civilian London and the use of poison gas at Ypres in Belgium. Their unrestricted submarine warfare against commercial shipping was considered barbaric and a challenge to neutral America's freedom of the seas. Wilson's tireless efforts to end the war proved futile, and the American Preparedness Movement that Hobey and others were taking part in gained momentum. On January 26, 1917, the president asked Congress for authority to arm US-flagged merchant vessels so they could take military action to protect American commerce.

The Preparedness Movement was championed by prominent Republicans and Harvard alums, Theodore Roosevelt and Henry Cabot Lodge. The movement, charged with "jingo fever" and "newspaper patriotism," brought America one step closer to war. Lodge had proposed years earlier that gentlemanly athletics was a substitute for preparation for war and a remedy for the "man of action" hopelessly trapped in an office. General Leonard Wood, the Army's Chief of Staff, opened a "businessmen's military training camp" at Plattsburg, New York so desk-bound warriors could prepare to demonstrate their Saxon chivalry.

A German diplomatic blunder known as the Zimmermann Telegram was the catalyst that finally drove neutral America over the top. The German high command had recently resumed its policy of unrestricted submarine warfare after a brief hiatus that was intended to temporarily appease the United States. Germany feared that this reinstatement of the detested policy would push the Americans toward the Allied cause. German Foreign Minister Alfred Zimmermann attempted through diplomatic actions to draw the United States into an armed conflict with Mexico and Japan, which would provide a distraction for America while affording the Germans the time needed to achieve victory on the Western Front. Through their ambassador in Washington, D.C., the Germans proposed the desperate plan to the Mexicans. If they would declare war on the United States, Germany would assist Mexico in the re-conquest of Texas, Arizona and New Mexico. Japan would be induced by the German government to join in the war against the United States.

Unfortunately for the Germans, Woodrow Wilson had recently improved relations with Mexico before the telegram arrived, and President Carranza of Mexico rejected the proposal. To make matters worse for the Germans, the telegram was intercepted and decoded by the British Admiralty Intelligence Service, and it was promptly sent to Woodrow Wilson. An enraged Wilson published the Zimmermann Telegram and on April 2, 1917, stood before Congress to ask for a declaration of war on Germany. The vote was taken on April 6th and America was at war. President Wilson told his nation and the world that this would be a fight for the ultimate peace of the world and declared, "The world must be made safe for democracy." He then sadly remarked to his personal assistant that his speech was "a message of death to our young men." The president was painfully aware that by the end of 1916 the French and British armies had suffered almost six million casualties, and the German casualties were approaching three and a half million men. He was sending the pride of America into the living hell known as the Western Front.

Hobey Baker had trained for this day for over a year, and like many young men across the nation was anxious to sail to Europe and fight the terrible "Hun." On August 23, 1917, he sailed with the first group of pilots to be sent overseas. The Selective Service Act of 1917 was signed into law on May 18th and over the next two years 23.9 million men would register for the draft. Almost three million men would eventually be drafted. In the case of Hobey, no draft legislation was necessary. Just as Harvard alums, Alan Seeger and Edward Mandell Stone, the first American to lose his life in World War One, had made the supreme sacrifice fighting in the French Foreign Legion before the United States entered the war, hundreds of sons of Princeton, Harvard and Yale were now anxious to fulfill their *noblesse oblige* and to join with Americans from all walks of life in making the world safe for democracy. As soon as the president declared war, Princeton's enrollment stood at forty percent of the previous peacetime year, and five Tigers a week were leaving for the front. Few Americans were aware that with the exception of Annapolis and West Point, the sons of Nassau gave a larger portion of their student body to the military than any other institution. As Hobey sailed for Europe in one of the first ships to transport Americans to the Great War, he thought of his former classmate at St. Paul's, Victor Emmanuel Chapman, who had lost his life in the Lafayette Escadrille in June of 1916, while assisting several comrades who were outnumbered in a vicious dogfight. Chapman's fellow pilot, Norman Prince, wrote to Chapman's family that Victor's was a, "glorious death, face *a l'ennemi,* for a great cause, and to save a friend." America's most famous athlete pondered his own fate as his ship drew closer to the war-torn continent.

The Lafayette Escadrille fought in the vicious air battles over the "killing fields" of Verdun. The average life of a World War I fighter pilot was only two weeks. The battle-scarred village seen from an Escadrille air-machine after the horrific shelling that began on February 21, 1916.

And we won't come back 'til it's over Over There

George M. Cohan

Chapter Ten

There were three classes of aircraft used in the Great War in Europe. The first consisted of small, single-seated planes commonly referred to as pursuit or scout machines. These were the English *Sopwith Camel*, French *S.P.A.D.* and *Nieuport*, and German *Pflaz*, *Albatross* and *Fokker*. One of Hobey's fellow pilots joked that while they were officially assigned to a pursuit group, they were often the pursued.

The second group of planes was the larger aircraft used for reconnaissance and to direct the placement of the deadly artillery attacks. This type of machine carried at least two men. The third was the multi-engine bombers that carried a crew that could vary from two to eight men. No pilots of any class of airplane carried parachutes as they were considered untested, unsafe and not for official issue.

The small, single-engine pursuit planes were the fastest and could reach speeds of 135 miles per hour. While occasionally called upon to drop small bombs or to launch primitive air-to-air rockets at enemy observation balloons, their primary purpose was to fight the enemy's pursuit planes in order to provide safe passage for their own larger aircraft. They were armed with one or two synchronized machine guns that employed a cam to enable them to shoot through the propeller without tearing it apart. The procedure employed to shoot down an enemy plane was in theory uncomplicated, but in reality a nightmare. A pilot was required to aim his plane at his enemy, frame the other aircraft in his sites and start firing the machine gun by pressing a trigger that was attached to the gun by a series of cables. Since the plane carried only one pilot, it was completely vulnerable from the rear where more often than not, the enemy was framing it in his sites. If that wasn't enough to keep a fledgling airman on the ground, there was the ever-present, deadly German anti-aircraft fire called *Archies* so named by the British pilots, after a popular London dancehall musical of the day. In the final song of the wartime favorite, the heroine would sing out, "Archibald, certainly not!" as she fended off the lecherous villain. A young British pilot shouted, "Archibald, certainly not!" as some enemy ground fire came too close to his plane, and the name stuck and spread throughout the Allied squadrons.

Guns often jammed and a dogfight usually lasted a few brief moments with each machine flying at high speeds. Engines were unpredictable causing one of Baker's comrades to comment that he pitied the more mechanically inclined pilots because they would become frozen from fear upon recognizing that a particular ping or an odd moan emitting from the engine suggested that the 220 horses were about to give up the ghost. He preferred to patrol the skies in a state of ignorant bliss.

The air-service and the life of a pursuit pilot attracted men of Hobey's background for a variety of reasons. The transformation from a killer of athletic records to a killer of men can be understood when the philosophy of the gentleman athlete is observed. Play to win but play by the rules. Honor meant more than victory to men like Baker and Alan Seeger, and sadly the slaughter in Europe had begun more as a test of national character than an advancement of national interest. The vanishing culture of character had run head-on into twentieth century technology and death on an unimaginable scale.

A Yale alum who also served as a pursuit pilot commented that he was attracted to flying because of the romantic appeal. That was easy to understand. The "old boy" club of American pilots consisted primarily of men from the best eastern seaboard schools who had played sports together, and should they survive the war, they would become members of the same exclusive clubs and run the country as their fathers and grandfathers had. There was also a gentlemanly aspect to the Air Service that appealed to these men born into a life of privilege. A pilot wrote home that he chose not to lead men into the inevitable slaughter of the trenches, but desired a life where you profited from your own skill or suffered from your own mistakes. While Hobey excelled at team sports, he always chose the role of the solitary warrior: the independent rover on the ice or the fearless punt return man on the gridiron. He, too, wished to succeed or fail based on his own merits. Statisticians estimated the average combat life expectancy of a pursuit pilot was approximately two weeks, yet Baker anxiously awaited his first combat assignment.

An Escadrille pilot wrote home that he and his comrades lived like princes when they were not "working." They were driven to their machines by automobile and strapped in securely by the mechanics crew who tended to the airplanes and pilots like the squires of a forgotten era. The motor would be put "en route" and they would be off for "two or three hours to prowl through the air, looking for an enemy machine to dive on and have it out with." It was not uncommon for a squadron commander to secure a spacious villa to house the men, sometimes complete with a gourmet chef. No army rations for these superstars of the heavens!

The first pilot of the Escadrille Americaine to shoot down a German plane was stationed in the French town of Luxeuil at the time of the incident. A fellow pilot commented that all Luxeuil smiled upon him, "especially the girls." Another comrade quickly sent to Paris for a bottle of eighty-year-old Bourbon, an extremely rare wartime treat, that they planned on drinking in his honor. After careful deliberation, they decided instead to ration the priceless nectar, one glass at a time, to celebrate each confirmed kill of the squadron. The joyful pilot drank his glass of Bourbon and the entire town celebrated in his honor. Lieutenant Hobey Baker and the newly arrived pilots had read of the daring exploits of the Escadrille and were anxious to claim their first "Hun."

Baker was initially disappointed to discover upon his arrival in Europe in August 1917, that he would not be assigned a fast machine and sent immediately to the front. He was first assigned to a desk in Paris, and from there he was required to be brevetted or certified in the French flying schools at Avord, Cazau, and Pau. Avord was the largest aviation school in France, where new pilots were trained on *Penguins*, Bleriot monoplanes with wings cut down so they could not get off the ground. The object of the *Penguin* course was to teach the recruits to handle the stick, to steer straight and to roll correctly at speeds of up to forty miles an hour. Hobey wrote his father of his disappointment and compared his combat delay to having the Yale game put off for a year the day before it was to be played. He was frustrated but understood the necessity of the military training and mentioned in the same letter home that Julian Biddle, a friend of his from Philadelphia, had been sent to battle in a French unit only half-prepared and was killed his first week at the front. Hobey also noted that with so many classes taught in French, his success depended on how quickly he could pick up the language. It was obvious to him that the Americans were three years behind the French and British aviation services and would probably not get up to speed for at least a year. After completion of the *Penguin* training, he was next instructed on a *Rouleur*, a Bleriot which although it could fly, was not permitted to leave the ground.

The object of the *Rouleur* was to teach the pilot to achieve a correct *ligne de vol* (line of flight). Next was the *Decolleur,* which permitted the *eleve pilote* (student pilot) to fly about three to six feet from the ground in a straight line.

Hobey next graduated to *Nieuports,* quick aircraft that the students used to take the final French Brevets. As the drills grew faster and were performed at higher altitudes, they became more dangerous. In a letter from Avord he mentioned to his family that there was an average of four smashes a day at the school. Like any athletic challenge Hobey ever attempted, and flying a primitive aircraft required immense athletic ability, success came easily and he completed the dangerous course. He was now a *pilote aviateur.* After Avord he was sent to Paris where he awaited the arrival of two hundred mechanics from the United States whom he was to assume command of and accompany to the school at Pau. Bored and restless, he took long walks and rented a boat and rowed the river with friends to stay in shape. He wrote Percy at home that he didn't expect to see the front before mid-winter or the spring.

Hobey left Paris for Pau by train with his mechanics in tow and anxiously anticipated his next step in becoming a full-fledged pursuit pilot: acrobatic flying. On the all-night train ride to Pau, he rode in a compartment with a French family. The daughter was young and pretty, but the language barrier made his attempts at conversation impossible. He spent the long journey watching her fall in and out of sleep, happy to be in the presence of such a beauty.

The pilots stayed in the town of Pau and were sent to the school five miles away via a train-trolley each day. The young flyer experienced tragedy first-hand when an American whom he had befriended at Avord was killed in training at Pau. Each day another accident would occur, as the French put the knights in training through their vigorous classes. There was no time to spare so on rainy days the students were driven by truck to a machine gun range where they would sit in mock airplane cockpits firing at targets with German planes painted on them. Hobey scored a high percentage of hits, but always modest he wrote home that he would do better with practice.

By the end of September, Baker was concerned that he would never leave the school at Pau. While effortlessly excelling at his classes, he could not shake the two hundred mechanics whom he had inherited and now commanded. He prayed that another American officer would come along and take charge. He was now training in group formation flying and especially enjoyed the daily two-hour flights in the speedy, *Nieuports* across the beautiful countryside. His lack of French was not only a problem with pretty girls on trains. He wrote a friend that the beautiful autumn flights were marked by his fear that he had no way of requesting assistance from the locals should a forced landing be required. Another friend was killed during a training exercise, and as Hobey attended his comrade's funeral, he was unaware that he would come close to losing his own life three weeks later.

To increase shooting accuracy, the pilots were required to attack a target, towed by another plane at seventy-five miles per hour. The trainee would dive on the target at speeds exceeding one hundred miles an hour, shooting his fixed machine gun while attempting to avoid colliding with the tow-plane. The trick was to get as close as possible to the target, shoot the gun and pull away just in time to clear the cable and target. That day as Hobey's plane dove on the target at 7,000 feet, one of his bullets struck the tow-line causing the sleeve-like target to wrap around his landing wheels and the line itself to snap off most of his propeller. The mishap sent his craft into a deadly, downward spiral. As he lost altitude, he cheated death by only seconds, pulling the damaged plane out of the spin, and gliding it onto the field just as the target tore loose from his wheels. When describing the incident to a friend, he wrote that he was extremely sorry to break the machine and added, "...I thought for the first minute that I was about to be killed and it did not seem to worry me." Hobey was proud that he had kept his head and done exactly what was necessary to safely land the machine, as on the average two airplanes a day were destroyed by bad landings.

Eventually he was liberated from the mechanics at Pau, and after attending and graduating from the machine gun school in Cazau, he returned to Paris as a fully qualified pursuit pilot. Ready for action and hoping to connect with one of the French Escadrilles, he was discouraged to discover that he was to be sent to England and then to the desolate air base at Issoudum, France to teach eager Americans what he had just learned. While awaiting orders, he spent his days flying from a nearby airfield, dining with friends in Paris and occasionally attending one of the regular parties thrown by Cole Porter, who was holding court in Paris, wearing a bogus custom-made uniform in order to impress his guests and convince them that he was actually in the service.

By November 12th Hobey was at the Regent Palace Hotel in London, waiting to enter the Instructors School at Gosport, England. With language no longer a barrier, he spent his time, as he wrote a friend, "having tea at some crazy Lord's house and courting an English girl." He longed for the action at the front and was experiencing difficulty living on non-combat pay in an expensive city. Hobey suspected that he was running out of time to make a success of himself in the Air Service, but he had no idea that the war would end in a year almost to the day that he had arrived in London.

Part of Baker's training at the Instructors School was in the latest methods employed to create new pilots for the front as fast as possible. He flew with his pupils in a "double seater aero" and communicated with them via a telephone connection. His frustration at not being sent to the front was tempered by the fact that he was also honing his flying skills while instructing the recruits. He wrote to his father that he couldn't understand the English flyers' lack of enthusiasm and that he was forced to curb his excitement for battle in their presence. He added in the same letter, "I certainly would hate to come home without having done any real work at the front, but if I do I can come with the feeling I made my best efforts to get out there." He spent his last few days in England flying as often as possible and wrote in a letter that while the days were dark and gloomy he loved the bright, gleaming sunshine above the clouds for it reminded him of "some great plain covered with drifting snow." Just as he left the school at Gosport, he attended a lecture where a pilot advised that they would probably not last long at the front, and the weary athlete wished he could see his home and family one more time before beginning combat. He left the school for London and before heading to France raised his spirits with a swim at the Royal Automobile Club and about fifteen holes of golf. The next day he met friends for dinner at the Carlton, attended the theatre and called it an early night.

He spent a few days in Paris until he was ordered to proceed to the airfield at Issoudum. Just as he settled in at the base, he was sent on an unexpected five-day leave to Biarritz. As he relaxed at the Hotel Du Palais, he found himself wondering where his journey would eventually take him. There was a rumor that the leave was a prelude to a trip to the front. The natural athlete in him emerged for a brief moment when a friend from the Ambulance Service invited him to play golf while in Biarritz. Out of practice, he was down by four with six to go when, as he later wrote Percy in New York, "I suddenly started hitting everything and beat him one up." Next, in a letter sent home from a hotel in Bordeaux, he told his family that a rumor about his advancing to the front was false and that he was very discouraged. He spent Christmas in Pau at a dinner with English and American aviators.

By New Year's he was one step closer to the front, flying mock combat exercises with Eddie Rickenbacker and a college friend, Seth Low, Jr. His letters home began to reveal a recklessness that could prove fatal in actual combat. He boasted of almost driving Seth Low into the ground while on his tail in a high-speed simulated battle. In another incident he was flying without his hat or goggles, firing on a balloon in an aerial exercise. The powder from his machine gun temporarily blinded him, and he flew straight into the balloon. It wrapped around his wing and caused a drag. His plane hit the ground in a tailspin and flipped on its back. He totaled the plane but miraculously walked away with a minor head wound.

February of 1918 found Hobey in the Hotel Edward in Paris convinced that he would never see action. Writing to Percy back in America, he said that he would die of old age or be killed by a Parisian taxi before going to the front. The problem was that there was a shortage of airplanes, guns and ammunition, and every order to proceed to the front was countermanded almost immediately. The hopeful warrior realized that with America in the war there could be an Allied victory before he ever claimed his first German plane.

On a bright note, Hobey mentioned in the same letter that he was seeing Mimi Scott, a "nice girl" who had put her debutante lifestyle on hold in November of 1917 and volunteered to serve with the Red Cross in an evacuation hospital in France. Hobey had met Miss Jeanne Marie (Mimi) Scott in the United States through his brother Thornton. Just as with Percy Pyne, Baker's fame as an athlete, along with his movie star good looks, allowed him to travel in Mimi's exclusive circle. She was the "It Girl," a fabulously wealthy socialite heiress who spent summers in Newport, Rhode Island and the rest of the year at her Fifth Avenue townhouse in New York City or in fashionable Palm Beach in sunny Florida. Mimi was one of the most photographed society girls in America, and she made her formal debut into that society at a dance at the Newport Clambake Club during the summer of 1914, the same year that Hobey had graduated from Princeton. The New York newspapers unanimously praised Mimi for "abandoning all of her social duties during the winter season of 1916-1917" and enrolling in a crash course in nursing. A wartime romance developed as the couple spent time together in Paris whenever Mimi's 10-day "permission" or leaves from the front would permit. Hobey awaited his orders and was deeply embarrassed when he discovered that several newspapers back home had published erroneous stories concerning his wartime heroics. The press could never get its fill of the young star on the ice or gridiron, and if he hadn't yet seen any action, no matter; a few unscrupulous editors created the sensational headlines his public clamored for back home. One report had him shooting down his sixth German plane, and the ribbing he took from the more war-seasoned pilots caused him to curse his sensational "newspaper name." He even went so far as to write a French newspaper, demanding an explanation as to why it had published an erroneous report of his shooting down "another Bosch." On another occasion Baker discovered that his father had supplied the *Princeton Alumni Weekly* with sections of several letters he had sent home and begged him to never do it again. "Please Father," he begged. "I have enough notoriety now, and people over here do nothing but kid me and make me feel that I had a hand in every rumor of me bringing down Boche." Hobey hated the fact that his celebrity status sold newspapers and felt even more pressure to prove himself in battle.

His wish finally came true, and in April of 1918 Lieutenant Hobart Amory Hare Baker was assigned to the 103rd Aero Squadron that had been formed from the legendary Lafayette Escadrille. In January 1918, William Thaw, one of the surviving founding members of the Escadrille, had been commissioned a major in the United States Army Air Service, and on February 18, 1918, the Lafayette Escadrille was absorbed into the United States military. Baker would finally see action and with one of the most legendary escadrilles in the war.

Hobey was happy to serve under Flight Commander

Charles Biddle, a fellow Princeton Tiger. Biddle wrote in
his flight diary that he had taken the noted athlete on his
first flight over the lines on April 12th. He taught his charge
how to find Huns and compared the search to hunting wa-
terfowl, a lifelong hobby that had taught Biddle to carefully
scan the skies and see things that other pilots often missed.
Biddle attributed his having never been surprised by the
enemy in the air, an event that cost many a pilot his life, to
his love of duck hunting. The French referred to a pilot's
ability to see the sky in this great detail as "vision of the air."
Biddle and his student crossed the enemy lines at about
3,000 meters and were immediately attacked by anti-aircraft artillery. Appearing as spots of black all around their
planes, the *Archies* almost lifted Hobey out of his seat, but all
he could think about was that he was finally "doing active
work." Hobey liked and respected Biddle and witnessed the
more experienced flyer take down a German plane on that
first flight. He watched at close range as Biddle, Princeton
alum and Harvard attorney, riddled the pilot of the twin-
seater with machine gun fire and then closed in and killed
the helpless observer sending both men to their deaths.
The Ivy League boys had become hired killers and both
relished the hunt. Biddle noted in his journal that Baker's
courage was beyond question and believed he had the right
instincts to become a successful pursuit pilot. Hobey wrote
his father after that first day and ended his letter with, "Yes,
I was scared up there today," but concluded that " there
couldn't be a nicer way to die, quick, sure and certain."

Hobey continued to see Mimi whenever they both
had a break from the front and wrote his father that she
would "certainly do for a wife." The celebrity flyer was smit-
ten with the socialite and believed that she was "real from
start to finish in spite of the fact that her life had been New
York, Palm Beach and Newport."

Baker completed the standard "In case of death or
accident sheet," listing his brother Thornton as family contact and took out a $10,000 life insurance policy with his

brother as beneficiary and instructions to pay the proceeds to his mother. He wrote Percy, "Well this at last is the front," and was living the storybook life of a daring aviator, courting danger daily and Mimi Scott whenever he could. In the same letter he admitted to his friend that he had a "real thrill" for Mimi and added, "Wouldn't it be queer if I lived through the war and tried to get her to marry me?" Reality sadly hit home as he closed with a somber, "What in the 'ell I would marry her on I don't know."

A killer with Ivy-League manners: Hobey wrote home to his father that he dreamed of encountering enemy aircraft while on patrol. While many flyers hoped for an uneventful patrol, Hobey craved action and compared air battles to a big game with Yale.

A young Apollo, golden-haired,
Stands dreaming on the verge of strife,
Magnificently unprepared
For the long littleness of life

Frances Cornford

Chapter Eleven

On August 21, 1918 Hobey wrote home that he was flying daily over the German lines and was enjoying every minute of it. He and Charles Biddle had pursued five biplanes over the Germans at Laon until a battery of anti-aircraft guns sent the two eager pursuit pilots scurrying almost fifteen kilometers to reach the Allied lines. This was not a career for the faint at heart. As difficult as the infantrymen's lives were, most respected and marveled at the courage of these men that would ride "flying egg crates" thousands of feet above the trenches, hunting and being hunted. Dueling to the death in the air took a rare kind of courage, and the same fearlessness that drove Hobey again and again toward the goal line or through a battery of lethal defensemen on the ice, now fueled his life of high adventure.

Hobey had met Raoul Lufbery and like most new pilots revered him, since as an original member of the Lafayette Escadrille, he had seventeen confirmed kills. Lufbery was assigned to the 94th Aero Squadron as an instructor when the Escadrille was absorbed into the United States Air Service. He was well-loved and while fearless, he was also very careful. He attributed his longevity in the air to this caution. Two years in a game that marked life expectancy in weeks seemed a lifetime.

On the morning of May 19, 1918, Lufbery's legendary luck ran out as he pursued a German reconnaissance airplane flying over the 94th Squadron's airfield. Lufbery's seventeen kills had all been over the German lines so he had never seen the wreckage of his victims. This would be his opportunity to take down an enemy plane over American lines in view of many of the pilots and staff on the ground who idolized him, and he uncharacteristically took off in a borrowed airplane as his was out of commission. He skillfully attacked the German *Albatross*, and just as his eighteenth victory was within his grasp, the unknown machine that carried him burst into flames. The crowd below watched with horror as the great hero chose jumping to his certain death rather than burning up in the flame-engulfed plane. Flying over 120 miles an hour, he jumped with no parachute from a height of two hundred feet and landed in the garden of a small farmhouse. Hobey wrote his father about Lufbery's death and lamented in the same letter that the British now had so many planes in his sector that the "Bosch won't come out." Nothing, not even Lufbery's horrific death, seemed to deter the anxious warrior.

On May 21st Hobey came close to bringing down his first enemy plane. He and five of his comrades flew into a nest of over thirty German planes, and before long a vicious dogfight erupted. The enemy aircraft were flying at heights between 3,000 and 5,000 meters so that Hobey found himself in the dangerous position of flying below some and above others. He dove on the tail of a large *Albatross* and let his machine-gun run steadily, discharging over 150 rounds. He suddenly discovered that a German tri-plane was on his tail. While diving and twisting to elude his pursuer, he found another *Albatross* and attacked him. As the six Americans were about to be swamped, a group of British *Dolphins* and French *S.P.A.D.'s* came to the rescue. He didn't receive confirmation that he had scored a victory until later that day and wrote his father that he was, "wild with joy."

To receive a confirmation on a "kill" was not a simple matter. The French regulations required that a pilot's claim be either corroborated by an observer on the ground or by an independent aerial observer not connected with the squadron making the claim. With so many dogfights taking place over German lines, it was impractical to expect Allied observers either on the ground or in the air to be present to witness the action. It was also common for more than one pilot to claim the "kill," and French observers were partial to French aviators. Many pursuit pilots felt that their tallies would have been much higher had it not been for this complicated and sometimes political system.

Hobey's victory was apparently rescinded, yet he still wrote home that the battle was the "biggest thrill I ever had in my life." He could not come down from the adrenalin high and compared it to the way he felt "after a big game." The excited flyer wrote that the battle had looked like wild pictures of air battles you see at home in magazines. He proudly described the chaos of the dogfight:"….machines in every manner of contortion. Some with the wheels pointing up instead of down, some climbing steeply in big turns, some diving with another on his tail." He ended the letter, "It was so exciting I forgot to be scared."

Hobey seemed oblivious to the death and danger that surrounded his new "sport" and was so elated the night after the battle that he could not sleep and missed the early morning patrol. The Americans met a group of eight Germans, and another terrific fight ensued. To Hobey's regret, he missed the action. Only three of the five American pilots returned to the airbase.

In between flights the men would spend time writing home to family and friends, swimming at the beach or visiting fellow soldiers and airmen at the other military facilities. Hobey seemed happy only when he was in the air.

The adventure continued. On one occasion, when

a sudden storm rolled in from the sea, he found himself separated from his squadron over enemy lines This was not an unusual event considering that the primitive navigation equipment consisted of a map and an often unreliable compass. By the time he came out of the clouds, he discovered he was only 200 feet above the German lines, and he was forced to play a deadly cat and mouse game, darting in and out of the mist to get his bearings while being greeted by a barrage of *Archies* each time he showed himself.

He continued his romance with Mimi Scott but grew more and more concerned about his prospects after the war. "I wish she did not have so much money and I more," he wrote his father in a letter home. He was saving his meager aviator's pay but pondered in the same letter, "What will I do if I live through this war?" His chances for survival were low. His squadron had lost three men in three weeks in May of 1918. Despite the daily danger, he wrote Percy, "I wish you could see how bold I am." He was given partial credit for a "kill" and was awarded the Croix de Guerre, the coveted French medal for heroism.

In June, Hobey was in the American Sector and spent three days in Paris with Mimi. He described the time as the most wonderful thing that had happened to him in a long while. He was very much in love with the young socialite, but upon meeting Mimi, a friend witnessed another side of her. Fifty years later, Charles Biddle, Hobey's flight commander, friend and roommate, described in a letter a lunch in Paris in 1918 where Hobey had introduced him to Mimi. His impressions of her were as follows: "She was a good-looking girl in a flashy sort of way - what the French would call chique (sic) - - but my impression of her was that she was hard and had no sweetness. To me she had no charm at all and I remember being very dubious about Hobey's prospects for happiness if he should marry her." He added that he realized his fellow aviator had fallen for Mimi so he concealed his disappointment in her.

During that summer Charles Biddle was put in command of the 13th squadron and requested that Hobey be assigned to the squadron as a Flight Commander. The St. Mihiel sector where they were stationed was quiet at the time, and the 13th Squadron spent its time training new pilots in preparation for the major offensive that everyone expected in the autumn of 1918. Baker had mixed feelings about the transfer. He felt that he had not had the time to "made good" at the 103rd, but felt that Biddle must have believed in him or he would not have requested Hobey as one of his commanders. That confidence was well placed for on July 20th, Hobey and two of the men under his command brought down a German bi-plane and so his flight became the first one to score a victory for the 13th Squadron.

Although Baker possessed the talent, determination and courage to be as successful an aviator as American ace Eddie Rickenbacker or Raoul Lufbery, he was not blessed with the luck of being in the right place at the right time. In August of 1918, just before the major American-led St. Mihiel and Meuse-Argonne Offensives, Hobey and another pilot were rewarded for their ability and service and were appointed commanders of their own squadrons. Baker arrived ahead of the other new commander so he was the first to leave the 13th Squadron, and to his disappointment, the action at the front. He was transported to the rear to organize the 180 enlisted men and twenty-six pilots who would comprise his new 141st Squadron and eventually return to the front in time for the critical offensives. The other squadron leader left shortly after Hobey.

As Charles Biddle would later write about Baker's experience with the new squadron, "He just struck rum luck from the start." From a bureaucratic standpoint, whatever could go wrong, did. By the middle of October, Hobey's squadron had still not received its airplanes or pilots, and he was forced to sit and wait. Although the pilot from the 13th Squadron who was promoted along with Hobey was sent to the rear to organize his new squadron weeks after Hobey had already left the front, his pilots and more importantly, his airplanes, arrived weeks before Baker's, and his squadron made it back to the front in time for the major offensive and all of the action. As the *S.P.A.D.* aircraft became available, Hobey and one of his flight commanders would ferry them to the 141st temporary airfield.

The only seemingly bright spot for Hobey that enabled him to endure the endless delays in returning to the front with his new squadron was his ongoing romance with Mimi Scott. In September, while still waiting for his airplanes, Hobey wrote his father with the exciting news that he was engaged to Mimi. Overflowing with absolute joy, he told his father that he didn't quite know how he had put it across but that he did. He was anxious for his family to meet Mimi and enclosed a photograph with the letter.

The love-struck daredevil instructed Percy to sell a bond so he could buy his fiancée a ring, and with no airplanes in sight for his new squadron, he spent his spare time notifying friends and relatives of the engagement. The major newspapers in New York City and Philadelphia ran with the story. The headline read, "Hobey Baker, Aviator, To Marry Miss Mimi Scott," and the story described the love-match between the "Princeton athlete and his fiancée both serving in France." Mimi's grandmother, Mrs. George S. Scott, who was "passing the autumn at Belmead, her home in Newport," officially announced the match to society. Such was the celebrity of the two lovers that the reporter noted, "No recent engagement is of more interest to society in New York, Newport and in Paris."

In early October of 1918, Hobey received some additional good news: the 141st Squadron's airplanes had arrived. He promptly had them painted orange and black, his beloved Princeton colors, and each airplane carried the insignia of his new squadron, a powerful tiger mauling a German helmet. His men had been trained to perfection on other planes while waiting for their own to arrive and were now ready for their Princeton Tiger to lead them into battle. Hobey, recently promoted to the rank of captain, and his men finally made it back to the front at the end of October when they took their place at the Toul airdrome.

All reports indicate that Baker was a popular commander. His flight officers thought of him as fun-loving, self-effacing and always supportive. One wrote years later, "I never knew a more mature young man – completely well-balanced – a true gentleman." He was tough when required but always chose to lead by example. Sam Slaughter, a "green" pilot assigned to Hobey's squadron, recalled how his seasoned captain took him on his very first patrol. The new recruit was walking the base when Baker yelled for him to follow him. Both men jumped into their *S.P.A.D.'s* and headed for the lines. They encountered heavy anti-aircraft action but eventually returned to their base without encountering the enemy. When amused, Baker would emit a low chuckle followed by a broad grin. As they walked back to the barracks, Hobey flashed a boyish smile and handed Slaughter the message that had caused the two pilots to rush to the front. An Allied observation balloon crew had reported seeing eight German *Fokkers* in the vicinity and requested a patrol to intercept them. Hobey was unimpressed with the four-to-one odds and expressed regret that he and his new charge had not found the enemy.

Baker scored his second victory when in early November, while cruising twenty thousand feet above the lines, he encountered an enemy two-seater and instinctively attacked. He skillfully outmaneuvered the German machine and shot the pilot. The aircraft fell upside down for four or five thousand feet, and the observer fell from his seat to his death. Just as the plane was about to run out of altitude, the pilot came to, righted the aircraft and headed for the German lines. Hobey got on his tail and once again riddled the hapless pilot with machine gun fire and sent him spiraling to earth.

For Baker, the third victory occurred just a few days before the armistice on November 11th. It would be his last. The fearless warrior would never fulfill his potential as an ace pursuit pilot. The equipment delays that had prevented his 141st Squadron from returning to the front until late October kept him out of the action during the last full-scale offensive. There is no doubt that had he returned to the front in early September of 1918, he would have scored many additional victories. The great flying ace, Eddie Rickenbacker, scored twenty of his twenty-six victories between September 1st and October 30th when the sky was filled with enemy aircraft during the St. Mihiel and Argonne Offensives. Rickenbacker wrote in a letter forty years after the war that Hobey had been an outstanding pilot and noted that his delay in returning to the front cost Baker the coveted "ace" designation.

As the war ground to a halt, so did Hobey's love affair with the vacuous Mimi Scott. While Hobey was dreaming of returning to America and beginning his life with the young debutante, she had already moved on to her next lover. In his last letter home to his father, the heartbroken aviator wrote that he now believed that Mimi had only loved him until the "right one came along." The right one turned out to be Philander L. Cable, a wealthy diplomat stationed in Paris. Hobey lamented to his father that, "I am certainly good when it comes to girls." One newspaper that carried the original engagement announcement ran a two-paragraph story on November 26th entitled, "Their Troth Broken," while another society reporter announced that the match had been, "Dissolved by Mutual Consent of Athletic Star and Fiancee, Miss Mimi Scott." Hobey closed his final letter home by promising his father, "Someday, Father, I want to have a long talk with you about Mimi." That conversation would never take place.

The war officially came to an end at 11 AM on the 11th day of November 1918. On December 21, 1918, Hobey Baker received his orders to return home.

While a ticket home was the dream of every soldier who had been fortunate enough to survive the world's first global conflict, Hobey dreaded returning to the humdrum

Wall Street position that Percy Pyne had promised him. He admitted to a friend that he would give almost anything to have made it back to the front by the beginning of September instead of late October. Simply put – he had not had his fill of the danger and action that gave many of his comrades nightmares. He considered his three victories, his French Croix de Guerre and his citation for bravery from the American Expeditionary Force commander, General John Pershing as meaningless as his athletic achievements. He craved the excitement that could be achieved only on the stadium field or in a flying egg crate thousands of feet over the deadliest playing field of all.

December 21st was a gloomy day, having rained most of the morning. His three flight commanders were sitting around a glowing stove in their barracks, sipping a mixture of cognac and Benedictine and roasting chestnuts when the ebullient Captain Baker bolted in, smiling and waving his orders to return home. That morning Baker had driven with his motorcycle driver, Howard Nieland, to Toul to receive his orders to return home. A fellow pilot who had spotted Hobey returning to the airfield laughed when he realized that Baker's driver was relaxing with his feet up in the side-car while the commander drove the motorcycle. This was what the men had learned to expect from their "very democratic" captain. Baker had planned on taking the 8 PM train to Paris en route home, but this is the part of the story where it becomes impossible to separate fact from legend so I will present two versions of Hobey's death and let you, the reader, decide.

Raoul Lufbery was a pilot among pilots and one of the original members of the Lafayette Escadrille. Hobey Baker idolized Lufbery, who had seventeen confirmed kills. He was assigned to the 94ᵗʰ Aero Squadron as an instructor when the Escadrille was absorbed into the United States Air Service. His legendary luck ran out on May 19, 1918 in an air battle with a German Albatross.

Flying in World War One was as much an art as a science. Taking off at the Escadrille's airfield at Ham was at best a roll of the dice. Survival depended on a quick climbing takeoff with a sudden bank to the left as the fragile machine attempted to gain altitude. The field was located dangerously close to the tiny village of Eppeville, and an accident on takeoff would be a disaster for the population. It required a special kind of courage to attempt a take-off and landing from a mud-covered, primitive field like Ham. If a pilot was fortunate enough to become airborne, he soon encountered an enemy pilot attempting to shoot him down. It is easy to understand why these brave souls were known as the "knights of the air."

Charles Biddle, a fellow Princeton pilot, was Hobey's commander and was happy to take the eager pilot under his wing. The popular commander of the 103ʳᵈ Aero Squadron, formed from the legendary Lafayette Escadrille, took the famous athlete on his first mission over enemy territory. Biddle wrote in his journal that Baker's courage was beyond question and believed that Hobey had the right instincts to become a successful pursuit pilot. Charles Biddle survived the war, founded one of the most prestigious law firms in the country and lived to be eighty-two years of age.

Now you will not swell the rout
Of lads that wore their honours out,
Runners whom renown outran
And the name died before the man.

Alfred Edward Housman, *To an Athlete Dying Young*

Hobey's Death – *Version One*

In this popular and generally accepted version of the incident that claimed Baker's life, he announced to his envious buddies that he would take one last flight in his old *S.P.A.D.* before he left Toul for Paris and home. In unison, his three flight commanders implored their beloved captain not to tempt fate and to stay on the ground. A superstitious lot, many pilots believed that an unnecessary "last flight" might be just that. As Hobey approached the hangar, more men joined the group pleading with him to listen to reason. Undeterred and still in command, he called for his own plane, *S.P.A.D. No. 2*, to be brought out to the field. At the same moment a mechanic was wheeling out *No. 7*, a recently repaired plane whose carburetor had failed in flight a few days earlier. Unaware of the other squadron members' concerns, the mechanic suggested to his commander that he take the *No. 7*. As if the original slap in the face of superstition and tradition were not enough of an adrenalin rush for the handsome pilot, he decided to switch to a strange machine, *S.P.A.D. No. 7*. "I think I should test the repair," he announced to the anxious crowd that now surrounded him. "After all, the safety of the squadron is still my responsibility until I leave for Paris."

Whether it was recklessness, hubris, or just plain devotion to the 141st Squadron, he taxied the strange aircraft down the slippery runway, taking off into the bleak December sky. As he gained altitude, he attempted to execute what the French flyers called *a Chandelle,* an upward corkscrew climb. One of his fellow pilots would later describe the maneuver when made on take-off and near the ground as a "very risky piece of business and Hobey knew it." As he leveled off around six hundred feet, the unreliable carburetor failed and the motor cut out. A witness reported that Hobey could have taken advantage of the one saving grace the *S.P.A.D.* was known for, the ability to be pancaked into the most difficult terrain, allowing the pilot to walk away with minor injuries. Baker, like most seasoned pilots, knew this about the *S.P.A.D.* and had once crash-landed a similar aircraft on a farmer's field and walked away with a few bruised ribs. Charles Biddle, his old commander, later wrote that Baker scared everyone who witnessed the previous crash landing because he at first attempted to reach the airfield rather than take the plane down in the nearest field. Biddle noted that every experienced pilot knew not to attempt to reach the airfield if he was too close to the ground. Once flying speed is lost and the plane slips off on a wing, a pilot can do nothing until he has dived enough to regain flying speed. If the plane does not have enough altitude, it becomes a deadly race to try to regain speed before it slams into the ground. Pilots know that this type of accident is almost always fatal.

On that tragic winter day, Baker chose not to pancake the plane but to go for the airfield. As he made the turn back toward the hangar, he pushed his joystick forward to regain sufficient air speed. His friends watched in absolute horror as Hobey ran out of altitude and violently smashed the nose of the fragile aircraft into the ground. He was just a few hundred feet from the field and safety. In this version, Hobey, always one to tempt fate, preferred to go for the field rather than face the embarrassment of crash landing a machine only hours before he was to leave for Paris. The *S.P.A.D.* with its primitive controls and light-weight construction was often described by pilots as an extension of their own body. Hobey Baker was born with the ability to perform physical feats of almost mythical proportions, and perhaps he truly believed that he could will the plane to the airfield by some innate power. Unfortunately, he challenged the gods one too many times. The final four lines of the anonymous poem on his headstone document the popular version of the incident:

> *I think someday you may have flown too high,*
> *So that immortals saw you and were glad,*
> *Watching the beauty of your spirits flame,*
> *Until they loved and called you, and you came.*

All of the major newspapers throughout Europe and the United States ran the story of the courageous "last flight" of America's most famous athlete, killed at twenty-six years of age, while testing a repaired plane, his orders to return home found in his jacket pocket at the time of the accident. This was the only acceptable explanation to his many fans, especially to the old Princeton guard.

"...grown up to find all Gods dead,
all wars fought, all faiths in man shaken...."

F. Scott Fitzgerald, *This Side of Paradise*

Hobey's Death – *Version Two*

This version is much more controversial and considered blasphemy by the eastern establishment. The details are the same up until the moment the engine grinds to a halt. Hobey, dreading the return to civilian life and broken-hearted over the loss of Mimi Scott, chooses another path. Knowing full well that he is not suited for the world of business and unsure of his future, he kills the motor and intentionally crashes the *S.P.A.D.* nose first into the bleak, frozen field.

This version, which at first seemed implausible, evolved from a kernel of suspicion sowed by witnesses to the crash. It is still debated over eighty years later. After all, when Kiffin Rockwell was killed in combat, flying with the famous Lafayette Escadrille, his hometown newspaper said, "He was one of those restless spirits to which life without adventure is but a sad and monotonous pilgrimage." Many pilots experienced a profound sense of loss on November 11, 1918, and some found it difficult to adjust to civilian life. Ernest Hemingway, who had volunteered as an ambulance driver during the war, developed a knack for putting himself in harm's way. He was injured by an Austrian trench mortar while spending time in a frontline listening post. Having survived the senseless slaughter, he spent years in the pursuit of post-war danger and the adrenalin rush he had experienced in Europe.

As his 1966 biography of Hobey Baker was about to go to press, author John D. Davies, who was also editor of the *Princeton Alumni Weekly*, wrote in a letter to Arthur Mizener, "I have tried to play down the suicide theory of his enigmatic death," and added that "some of the old guard would be furious if they thought I was trying to prove it." He did however state in his book that a relative of Hobey's could not imagine what Baker would have done after the war, believing that he was "far too fine a soul" to flourish in the world of business.

He was still young enough to play in a professional hockey league with one of the many teams that had attempted to recruit him before he left for Europe, and the money would have far exceeded his entry-level position salary on Wall Street. The great irony of his life was that his entire amateur athletic career prepared him for doing what his friends, social class and conscience would never permit: playing hockey or any other sport for money. He was taught from the first time he picked up a football or laced up a pair of skates that athletics were to be played by amateurs for the glory and love of the game. Hobey was a product of an elitist system that considered the "professional" a detriment to all sports. The year Baker graduated from Princeton, a plan to hire a resident football coach at the university was defeated because as *The New York Times* reported, "It smacks of professionalism."

Many years after Hobey's death, a member of the same graduating class recalled a chilling comment made by the famous athlete the summer Baker began flight instruction at Governor's Island. James Beck had invited Hobey to spend the weekend at his family's summer home in Sea Bright, New Jersey. As they enjoyed the sunshine and surf, their thoughts turned to their days at Princeton and they began to reminisce and laugh about their old friends and wonderful experiences. Hobey suddenly became uncharacteristically morose and told Beck that he realized his life was finished and that he would never experience the excitement of the gridiron or hockey rink again. The stunned friend believed that Baker already believed that his tragic death was not far off.

Although it would at first seem far-fetched that the break-up with Mimi Scott could have contributed to a possible suicide, Hobey's letters to his father and a life spent in all-male establishments without the warmth of a mother's affection point to a deeper attachment on his part to the careless debutante. While it was no more than a wartime amusement for Mimi Scott, Baker was deeply in love with her. In one letter home he discussed his engagement to Mimi and told his father that she was so much what he always wanted and added, "I feel all sorts of safe and happy." Living through the break-up of his self-absorbed parents and later shipped off to a prep school at eleven years of age, the man whom many contemporaries compared to an Adonis come to life, was longing for the tenderness and love of a good woman. His dream of a life with Mimi and the effect it would have on his dysfunctional family inspired him to write to his father in one of his last letters home, " I know it will be some day and then we shall all be so happy."

Before the engagement to Scott, Baker's letters home are riddled with comments questioning whether he would ever return from the war, and in one, written six months before his death, he referred to the possibility of losing his life in an airplane crash and ominously "...concluded that there couldn't be a nicer way to die, quick, sure and certain." In his book on the Lost Generation, *A Second Flowering*, author Malcolm Cowley discusses the death wish of many young men of Hobey's generation. "The possibility, almost the certainty, of being killed lent meaning and glamour to what might have been aimless lives," wrote Cowley.

Both versions of Hobey's tragic death end the same

way. His men ran to the stricken plane and pulled their beloved hero from the cockpit. There was little evidence of external damage with the exception of a small gash along his forehead that was partially hidden by his long blonde hair. His men gingerly placed him in an ambulance, but he never regained consciousness and died en route to the hospital at 11:55 AM. He was twenty-six years old. A friend commented that although Hobey daily drilled his men on the procedures that he had just ignored, he invariably took chances himself. "After all," recalled the fellow pilot fifty years after the accident, "Hobey was as near to being a superman as a human can get to be and he didn't live according to the book."

The sensational report of the death of America's most famous amateur athlete was carried in every major newspaper in Europe and the United States. One headline read: "Hobey Baker Was America's Athlete," with the subhead stating that he "possessed every qualification of a model competitor and sportsman." Just as eight decades later, so many strangers would mourn the meaningless, sensational accidental deaths of an English princess and the handsome heir to an American political dynasty, so did the fans of "America's Athlete," Hobey Baker, mourn his passing. And like Princess Diana and John Fitzgerald Kennedy Jr., he would remain forever young and beautiful in our collective memory.

As thousands of Americans learned of his death, many closed their eyes for a brief moment and pictured a happier time when this perfect athlete brought thousands to their feet on the football fields of Princeton, Yale or Harvard. One reporter remembered "rows upon rows in the stands, cheering thousands shrieking the name of a blonde-haired youth in the Princeton backfield – cheering the name of Hobey Baker." Others recalled the St. Nicholas skating rink packed to the rafters as they and thousands of other fans screamed until they were hoarse, watching their winged idol effortlessly carry the puck from goal to goal across the gleaming ice surface.

Hobey was buried next to two other fallen American pilots, Raoul Lufbery and David Putman, in a small military cemetery near Toul. Rain fell on the somber gathering of the 141st Squadron as they laid their beloved captain to his final rest. A group of generals and newspaper reporters made the trip to see the celebrity laid to rest. Someone sang, "Nearer my God to Thee," as the once perfect, but now broken body of the youth who even as a boy could astonish his fellow mortals with his athletic wizardry, was slowly lowered into his grave. Four days after the crash, the combination Christmas party and Armistice celebration for the 141st Squadron was still held, but one of Hobey's men would later remember that it was a somber event, as no one present could erase from his mind the death of the popular commander.

A ceremony was later held at Princeton University where six aviators from the War Department served as honor guards. University president, J. G. Hibben, delivered the memorial address at nearby Trinity Church before a group of several hundred students and friends of Baker. "He was the pride of the university," said Hibben. "We had hoped soon to welcome him home with his laurels and his honors, and it was with a passion of grief that the great company of his friends heard of his death." Hobey's body was returned to the United States in 1921, and he now lies buried in the West Laurel Hill Cemetery in Bala-Cynwyd, Pennsylvania.

They shall not grow old, as we that are left grow old.
Age shall not weary them, nor the years condemn
At the going down of the sun and in the morning
We will remember them.

Laurence Binyon

EPILOGUE

The world that Hobey Baker left behind on that bleak December day in 1918, when he lost his life in a final flight over the French countryside, had changed forever. Europe and America were left spiritually impoverished by the Great War, as the survivors came to realize that the millions of dead or maimed had been betrayed by their governments and the financiers and industrialists who had profited from the war. Instead of marching off to the great, decisive victories that their generals had promised them, brave and trusting men had been pawns in a horrific war of attrition. Disillusioned soldiers spoke out against their countries for leading so many men to their deaths believing that they were fighting a war of defense and liberation when in reality it was a war of aggression and conquest. The reparations and punishments the victors exacted on the Central Powers at the peace conference at Paris sowed the seeds for a century of conflict. Smaller nations that attended the conference in the belief that the Great War had been fought to make the world safe for democracy discovered that instead of bringing an end to colonialism, the war gave France, Italy and England a mandate for business as usual and the unchallenged expansion of their colonies. President Wilson's health failed, and he suffered a debilitating stroke as he attempted in vain to persuade the Congress to ratify the Treaty of Versailles and the Covenant of the League of Nations. Meanwhile, in Munich, an angry German soldier, who had been wounded during a gas attack in the battlefields of Ypres, questioned why so many of his countrymen had suffered and died in the humiliating defeat. His twisted mind searched for and invented a scapegoat. Adolph Hitler joined the anti-Semitic, German Labor Party as member Number 7.

The age of chivalry and the role of the gentleman warrior faded into the past century, monuments of a more genteel era. The world that Baker, the golden warrior, had conquered with such effortless poise and grace vanished almost overnight. A charter member of what Gertrude Stein would dub the Lost Generation, F. Scott Fitzgerald, a lifelong Baker admirer, would achieve fame as the scribe of the Jazz Age, a morally bankrupt period of America's history when personal gain and the pursuit of pleasure replaced many of the honorable traits that men like Hobey Baker and Alan Seeger had cherished. "It was not the Lost Generation which was lost," Pulitzer Prize winning poet Archibald MacLeish would say of that period after the war, "but the world out of which that generation came."

The ratification of the Eighteenth Amendment to the Constitution, prohibiting the sale, import, or export of liquor in the United States would soon fuel an unprecedented rise in crime and corruption. Thousands of soldiers would return home from the war and find it almost impossible to land a job or obtain a legal glass of beer. The year after Baker's death, 1919, would be marked by the country's first great sports scandal, the "fixing" of the World Series. The Black Sox Scandal, as it became known, seemed to epitomize post-war America. *The Chicago Herald and Examiner* reported the now famous line as a broken-hearted schoolboy pleaded with baseball legend Shoeless

Joe Jackson, one of the members of the Chicago White Sox, as his disgraced hero filed out of the courtroom. *"Say it ain't so, Joe. Say it ain't so."* Ironically, F. Scott Fitzgerald, who worshipped Baker as the vision come to life of the romantic, heroic athlete and incorporated him into several of his characters, would also immortalize another less noble acquaintance, Arnold Rothstein. Rothstein was rumored to have fixed the 1919 World Series, an act of betrayal so monumental that historian Eliot Asinof would describe it as "the telling incident in America's loss of innocence." In *The Great Gatsby*, Gatsby introduces Rothstein's fictional counterpart, Meyer Wolfsheim, to the naïve Nick Carraway as the man who fixed the series. When asked by Nick why Wolfsheim is not in prison, Gatsby replies, "They can't get him, old sport. He's a smart man." This was the era of the smart guy who did not play by the rules.

The romance and chivalry of Baker's era were flawed by a genetic blind spot to the rights of women, minorities and all people outside their social class. Still it was a culture of character that valued duty, honor, citizenship, and integrity above self. While their narrow concept of manhood may seem unenlightened and even frivolous in the twenty-first century, they genuinely sought to fulfill what they believed to be their *noblesse oblige* and to protect and spread civilization as they understood it. The officer class of all the armed services during World War I was almost exclusively comprised of these honorable men, all volunteers. Of the sixty thousand men lost by the British in just one day at the Battle of the Somme, the death rate was highest among young officers from the country's leading universities.

After the war, football and other sports took a giant leap toward becoming the national pastime for Americans of all social classes. The doughboys learned the game as they came into contact with the college athletes in their units and were eager to take the game to every corner of the country. Teams consisting of military men played in the Rose Bowl in Pasadena in 1918 and 1919, and although a

Crimson team went to the big game in 1920, the days when the big three – Harvard, Princeton and Yale – and the rest of the eastern football establishment dominated football, were numbered. Soon the country would be talking of the powerful Notre Dame teams coached by Knute Rockne and his "Four Horsemen," the backfield so named and immortalized by legendary sportswriter Grantland Rice, because they had crushed a lethal army team. With a few exceptions, such as the 1922 Princeton undefeated "team of destiny" or the 1950 Princeton team led by Heisman Trophy recipient and All-American, Dick Kazmaier, the Ivy Group was no longer a force to be reckoned with. By the middle of the twentieth century, unable and unwilling to compete with the national football dynasties that were powered by subsidies, athletic scholarships and massive enrollments, the Ivy League was officially created, and the Big Three along with the five other members de-emphasized football, and in a move that would have greatly pleased men like Hobey Baker, agreed to play by strictly amateur standards. This of course meant gridiron oblivion for the institutions that during Baker's era were the epitome of college football. The Ivy League schools believe that their emphasis on academics first is the reason that almost 95 percent of their athletes graduate, compared to the dismal 45-55 percent graduation rate of the modern collegiate football dynasties.

Today Hobey Baker is all but forgotten. Few current sons or daughters of Old Nassau know anything about Hobey. There is the Princeton University Hobart Amory Hare Baker Rink. Percy Pyne, Baker's close friend, spearheaded a campaign to raise funds to build a rink in honor of Princeton's most famous athlete shortly after Hobey's death. The university had no indoor rink of its own which indirectly added to Hobey's fame, as he and his teammates had been forced to play their season games in rinks in New York City, Philadelphia and Boston. A friend of Baker's, who had spent a season with him as young counselors at a summer camp near New York's Adirondack mountain range, told Pyne of a campfire conversation he had had with Baker one memorable August night. Each counselor had been asked what he would do if he suddenly received a million dollars. While the boys volunteered wild, age-appropriate ideas, Hobey's reply was direct and from the heart. "I would build the best skating rink I knew how," he told his campfire mates, "and have all my friends in to play hockey every day in the year." Pyne contributed $10,000 of his own money, and before the rink was dedicated on January 5, 1922, over 1500 college students and alumni from almost forty schools, plus Hobey's fans from all walks of life, made up the remaining $240,000. Harvard and Yale supporters contributed over 250 donations, and amateur teams like the St. Nick's and the Boston Athletic Association were happy to be part of the tribute to America's athlete. The inaugural game in the rink fittingly matched St. Paul's against Princeton. When it opened for the first game, it was the only indoor rink in the country owned by a university and used for intercollegiate play. Even in death, Hobey contributed to his beloved Princeton and the sport he had made famous, for before the rink was constructed the team often traveled hours just to play a half-hour practice at the old Ice Palace in Philadelphia. They were at a tremendous disadvantage to Harvard and the other teams, where natural conditions provided more opportunities to practice outdoors.

Another tribute to Baker is the Hobey Baker Memorial Award, established in 1981. The equivalent of the Heisman Trophy in college football, the award is presented each year to the individual voted best college hockey player in the country. While skill on the ice is naturally expected, the primary requirement, in honor of the award's namesake, is that the successful candidate must exhibit strength of character both on and off the ice. Some of the most sought after players in the National Hockey League today are Hobey Baker Memorial Award recipients.

Hobey achieved an honor that is not likely to be repeated: he is the only player to be enshrined in both the

College Football Hall of Fame and the Hockey Hall of Fame. He was the first American-born player inducted into the Hockey Hall of Fame, where he is also a charter member.

Hobey Baker was much more than the sum total of his achievements. In the years following his death, Princeton would produce other talented athletes but none with Baker's style and mystique. "He would drop-kick, tackle and run with a feline intelligence, grace and charm," wrote author John Tunis of the golden warrior. "He would make everything look so easy. Never was anybody else like Baker." Eddie Rickenbacker and other World War One pilots would tally more air victories than Hobey, but few inspired others as he did. Fearless yet fun-loving, he flew with the same style and panache that established his fame on the football field and hockey rink. He was what one fellow pilot remembered: "a different breed of cat."

We can only speculate how he would have played against today's hockey stars, but when Hobey skated, he was the show. His beautifully proportioned body, long blonde hair, and handsome features signaled the crowds that he was the one to watch. One spectator wrote of Baker's skating that he was "beauty wedded to strength."

While described as a "spectator's delight," by one of those fortunate enough to witness him play, what made Hobey memorable was his modesty and his dedication to playing by the rules, win or lose. He was cut from the same quality cloth that fashioned athletes like Joe DiMaggio, Lou Gehrig, Wayne Gretsky and Joe Louis. Their code was simple and immortalized by Grantland Rice in the lines:

When the One Great Scorer Comes
To mark against your name,
He writes not whether you won or lost,
But how you played the game.

For many years on the anniversary of Hobey's death, an unknown individual placed a red rose on his gravesite in Pennsylvania. Today the lonely plot, like Baker, is all but forgotten. The three hundred and twenty-five men of the Princeton class of 1914 are long gone. So are the scribes who witnessed, celebrated and documented Hobey's mythical feats on the ice and gridiron. Toward the end of his life, F. Scott Fitzgerald remarked that he would often dream that he had finally fulfilled his fantasy of becoming a football hero and fighting overseas in World War I. Charles Biddle, Hobey's air commander, lived to be eighty-two years old and his legacy, his law firm, is one of the most well-regarded practices in the United States. Percy Pyne went bust in the Stock Market Crash of 1929. Mimi Scott was wed six months after Baker's death to the diplomat she had met in Paris, Philander L. Cable. They all grew old and died, while the eternally young, beautiful athlete filled their dreams with images of lost youth and innocence.

December 21, 1918: the death of a hero and the birth of a legend

Select Bibliography

Books

American College and University Series, Princeton, Oxford
   University Press. 1914.

*An Undergraduate History of the Tiger Inn of Princeton, New
   Jersey, 1890-1940.* private printing at Princeton. 1940.

Asinof, Eliot. *1919, America's Loss of Innocence.* Donald I.
   Fine. New York, 1990.

Asinof, Eliot. *Eight Men Out.* Holt, Rinehart & Winston.
   New York, 1963.

Bederman, Gail. *Manliness and Civilization: A Cultural
   History of Gender and Race in the United States.* University of
   Chicago Press. Chicago, 1995.

Bergin, Thomas G. *The Game, The Harvard-Yale Football
   Rivalry, 1875-1983.* Yale University Press. New Haven,
   1984.

Biddle, Maj. Charles J. *The Way of the Eagle.* Charles
   Scribner's Sons. New York, 1919.

Bowen, Ezra. *Knights of the Air.* Time-Life Books. Alexandria, Virginia, 1980.

Brown, Rollo Walter. *Harvard Yard in the Golden Age.* A.A. Wyn. New York, 1948.

Carey, John, (editor). *Eyewitness To History.* Harvard University Press. Cambridge, Massachusetts, 1988.

Cowley, Malcolm. *A Second Flowering, Works and Days of the Lost Generation.* Andre Deutsch Limited. London, 1973.

Crichton, Judy. *America 1900, The Sweeping Story of a Pivotal Year in the Life of the Nation.* Henry Holt. New York, 1998.

Davies, John. *The Legend of Hobey Baker.* Little, Brown. Boston, 1966.

Deffaa, Chip, (editor). *F. Scott Fitzgerald: The Princeton Years, Selected Writings, 1914-1920.* Cypress House Press. Fort Bragg, 1996.

Edwards, William H. *Football Days, Memories of the Game and of the Men Behind the Ball.* Moffat Yard & Company. New York, 1916.

Farrington, S Kip, Jr. *Skates, Sticks and Men. The Story of Amateur Hockey in the United States.* David McKay Company. New York, 1972.

Ferrell, Robert. *Woodrow Wilson and World War I.* Harpers. New York, 1985.

Fitzgerald, F. Scott. *The Great Gatsby.* Charles Scribner's Sons. New York, 1925.

Fitzgerald, F. Scott. *This Side of Paradise*. Charles Scribner's Sons. New York, 1920.

Four American Universities, Harvard, Yale, Princeton, Columbia. Harper & Brothers. New York, 1895.

Goldstein, Richard. *Ivy League Autumns, An Illustrated History of College Football's Grand Old Rivalries*. St. Martin's Press. New York, 1996.

Haughton, Percy D. *Football, and How To Watch It*. Marshall Jones. Boston, 1922.

Heckscher, August. *A Brief History of St. Paul's School, 1856-1996*. The Board of Trustees of St. Paul's School. Concord, New Hampshire, 1996.

Heckscher, August. *St. Paul's, The Life of a New England School*. Charles Scribner's Sons. New York, 1980.

Hobart Amory Hare Baker – Occupation: Gentleman-Athlete. undated paper by Tristram Potter Coffin. University of Pennsylvania.

Kahn, Roger. *A Flame of Pure Desire, Jack Dempsey and the Roaring 20s*. Harcourt Brace. New York, 1999.

Keegan, John. *The First World War*. Alfred A. Knopf. New York, 1999.

Knowles, John A. *A Separate Peace*. MacMillian. New York, 1960.

Mason, Herbert Molloy Jr. *Lafayette Escadrille*. Konecky & Konecky. New York, 1964.

McCallum, John. *Ivy League Football since 1872*. Stein & Day.
New York, 1977.

Meyers, Jeffrey. *Scott Fitzgerald*. Cooper Square Press. New
York, 2000.

Miller, Linda Patterson, (editor). *Letters from the Lost
Generation, Gerald and Sara Murphy and Friends.*
Rutgers University Press. New Brunswick, New Jersey,
1991.

Mizener, Arthur. *The Far Side of Paradise, A Biography of F.
Scott Fitzgerald*. Houghton Mifflin. Boston, 1949.

Oriard, Michael. *Reading Football. How the Popular Press
Created an American Spectacle*. University of North Carolina
Press. Chapel Hill, 1993.

Pier, Arthur Stanwood. *St. Paul's School, 1855-1934*. Charles
Scribner's Sons. New York, 1934.

Preston, Diana. *Lusitania, An Epic Tragedy*. Walker &
Company. New York, 2002.

Princeton in the Great War. Princeton University Press.
Princeton, 1932.

Rice, Grantland. *The Final Answer and Other Poems*. A.S.
Barnes. South Brunswick, New Jersey, 1955.

Rickenbacker, Capt. Eddie V., *Fighting the Flying Circus*.
Doubleday, New York, 1965.

Rickenbacker, Edward V. *Rickenbacker, An Autobiography*.
Prentice-Hall. Englewood Cliffs, 1967.

Schreiner, Samuel A. *A Place Called Princeton*. Arbor House. New York, 1984.

Seeger, Alan. Letters and Diary. Charles Scribner's Sons. New York, 1917.

Seeger, Alan. Poems. Charles Scribner's Sons. New York, 1916.

Smith, Ronald A., (editor). *Big-Time Football at Harvard 1905: The Diary of Coach Bill Reid*. University of Illinois Press. Urbana and Chicago, 1994.

Smith, Ronald A. *Sports and Freedom: The Rise of Big-Time College Athletics*. Oxford University Press. New York, 1988.

Songs of Harvard. compiled by Lloyd Adams Noble, Hinds, Noble & Eldredge. New York and Philadelphia, 1914.

St. Paul's School in the Great War, 1914-1918. Published by The Alumni Association. 1926.

Susman, Warren I. *Culture as History, The Transformation of American Society in the Twentieth Century*. Pantheon. New York, 1984.

Thorn, John. *A Century of Baseball Lore*. Galahad Books. New York, 1980.

Townsend, Kim. *Manhood at Harvard, William James and Others*. W.W. Norton & Company, Inc. 1996.

Turnbull, Andrew. *Scott Fitzgerald*. Charles Scribner's Sons. New York, 1962.

Vanderbilt, Arthur T. II. *Fortune's Children, The Fall of the House of Vanderbilt.* William Morrow. New York, 1989.

Ward, Candace, (editor). *World War One British Poets.* Dover Publications. New York, 1997.

Ward, Geoffrey C., and Ken Burns. *Baseball, An Illustrated History.* Knopf. New York, 1994.

Watterson, John Sayle. *College Football, History, Spectacle, Controversy.* Johns Hopkins University Press. Baltimore, 2000.

Wharton, Edith. *Fighting France.* Charles Scribner's Sons. New York, 1915.

Manuscripts

Hobart A. H. Baker Papers
John Davies Collection
Seeley G. Mudd Manuscript Library
Princeton University

Newspapers/Periodicals

Boston Herald
Harpers
New Jersey Monthly
New York Evening Journal
New York Herald
New York Journal
New York Times
New York Tribune
Philadelphia Inquirer
Sports Illustrated
Sun (New York)

index

ABOUT THE AUTHOR

Emil Salvini is the author of the highly praised book, *The Summer City by the Sea, An Illustrated History of Cape May, New Jersey* (Rutgers University Press), and *Boardwalk Memories, Tales of the Jersey Shore* (The Globe Pequot Press).

Born in New Jersey, he is a graduate of William Paterson University and the Harvard Business School.

He lives with his wife, Nancy, in Wayne, New Jersey.